PEOPLE, PROCESS, AND PROFIT
A STRATEGIC HR APPROACH

DR. BARNANA BHATTACHARYA NANDY
DR. GAUTAMI CHATTOPADHYAY
DR. RINKI MISHRA

BLUEROSE PUBLISHERS
India | U.K.

Copyright © Dr. Barnana Bhattacharya Nandy, Dr. Rinki Mishra, and Dr. Gautami Chattopadhyay 2024

All rights reserved by author. No part of this publication may be reproduced, stored in a retrieval system or transmitted in any form or by any means, electronic, mechanical, photocopying, recording or otherwise, without the prior permission of the author. Although every precaution has been taken to verify the accuracy of the information contained herein, the publisher assumes no responsibility for any errors or omissions. No liability is assumed for damages that may result from the use of information contained within.

BlueRose Publishers takes no responsibility for any damages, losses, or liabilities that may arise from the use or misuse of the information, products, or services provided in this publication.

For permissions requests or inquiries regarding this publication,
please contact:

BLUEROSE PUBLISHERS
www.BlueRoseONE.com
info@bluerosepublishers.com
+91 8882 898 898
+4407342408967

ISBN: 978-93-6452-914-3

Cover Design: Sadhna Kumari
Typesetting: Pooja Sharma

First Edition: October 2024

Contents

Chapter 1: Fundamentals of Managerial Effectiveness 1
   Part 1: Introduction 2
   Part 2: Learning Managerial Capabilities 5
   Part 3: Problem Solving & Building Better Work Culture 9
   Part 4: Interpersonal & Group Behaviour 15
   Part 5: Role Of Global Managers 18

Chapter 2: Managing Diversity, Equity and Inclusion 22
   Part 1: Introduction 23
   Part 2: Understanding and Addressing Unconscious Bias 29
   Part 3: Introduction to Inclusive Culture 31
   Part 4: Diversity Recruitment and Hiring Practices 34
   Part 5: Equitable Talent Management and Development 36
   Part 6: Addressing Microaggressions and Workplace Conflict 38
   Part 7: Leveraging Employee Resource Groups (ERGs) for DEI 40
   Part 8: Measuring and Tracking DEI Progress 42
   Part 9: Leading with Empathy and Courage 43
   Part 10: Sustaining DEI Momentum and Overcoming Resistance 44

Chapter 3: Managing Employee Engagement 46
   Part: 1. Introduction 47
   Part 2: Theories of Employee Engagement 48
   Part 3: Factors Influencing Employee Engagement 55
   Part 4: Measuring Employee Engagement 58
   Part 5: Strategies for Enhancing Employee Engagement 61
   Part 6: Challenges in Managing Employee Engagement 66
   Part 9: Future Trends in Employee Engagement 70

Chapter 4: Leadership for Corporate Excellence 76
   Part 1: Introduction 77
   Part 2: Leadership Development and Skills 79
   Part 3: Leadership and Organizational Performance 81

Chapter 5: Data-Driven HR Strategy 85
- Part 1: Introduction to Data-Driven HR 86
- Part 2: The Evolution of HR: From Administrative to Strategic 88
- Part 3: Defining Data-Driven HR 90
- Part 4: The Future of Data-Driven HR 93
- Part 5: Advantages of Quantitative HR Data 95
- Part 6: Qualitative HR Data 95
- Part 7: Integrating Quantitative and Qualitative Data 97
- Part 8: The Role of Big Data in HR Management 102
- Part 9. Applications of Data-Driven HR 105
- Part 10: Predictive Analytics in HR 108
- Part 11: Tools and Technologies for Data-Driven HR 113
- Part 12: AI and Machine Learning in HR 114
- Part 13: Case Studies of Data-Driven HR Success 116
- Part 14: Future Trends in Data-Driven HR 120

Chapter 6: Fundamentals Of Critical Thinking 124
- Part 1: Introduction 125
- Part 2: Learning to Recognize Arguments 128
- Part 3: Basic Logical Concepts 132
- Part 4: Battle Of Bias 136
- Part 5: Framework And Models 142

Chapter 1: Fundamentals of Managerial Effectiveness

Part 1: Introduction

1.1 History

The role of managers has historically been challenging; however, recent developments over the past few years have exacerbated these difficulties. 2020 Workplace Scenarios indicated that a significant number of managers are facing performance challenges, as a result is impacting their direct performances. Furthermore, it revealed that a lack of supportive management may be a primary factor contributing to the departure of workers from their positions. To assist leaders in devising strategies to enhance managerial effectiveness,

The progression of managerial models throughout the twentieth century illustrates a significant increase in the complexity of a manager's role. In the early decades, Taylor (1911) and Fayol (1949) effectively characterized the work environment of the Industrial Revolution, depicting the manager as an individual who plans, organizes, commands, coordinates, and controls. However, the subsequent 25 years saw a growing acknowledgment of the social dimensions of work, leading to the emergence of human-relations models (Barnard, 1938; Mayo, 1933). These frameworks emphasized that managerial duties extended beyond mere productivity and efficiency, highlighting the importance of fostering positive human relationships.

1.2 What is Managerial Effectiveness?

Managerial Effectiveness pertains to the degree to which managers accomplish their intended outcomes within their groups/teams or departments. It encompasses individual's proficiency in establishing objectives, making informed decisions, communicating clearly, inspiring and motivating their team members, delegating responsibilities, and resolving conflicts. A manager's effectiveness is assessed by their capability to foster support and empower their direct reports, thereby influencing the organization positively. Key components of managerial effectiveness include managing performance, maintaining employee engagement, and setting and attaining goals at both individual and team levels, among other responsibilities.

1.3 Why is Managerial Effectiveness important?

Managerial effectiveness is an essential element of a thriving organization. Competent managers play a crucial role in realizing business goals and objectives as they coordinate efforts, guide team members, and ensure that tasks are executed effectively and efficiently. Moreover, these managers foster a productive, engaged, and positive work atmosphere, which enhances employee satisfaction and morale. Their leadership styles and practices directly impact employee retention, as effective management typically results in lower turnover rates. Additionally, their capacity to lead teams in adapting to changes and overcoming challenges significantly bolsters the overall resilience and competitiveness of the organization. Numerous issues currently affecting your organization can often be traced back to a single cause—ineffective management.

The adverse effects of underdeveloped or ineffective managers may include:

• High Turnover: Even well-intentioned managers lacking the skills to empower their teams can lead employees to seek opportunities elsewhere.

• High Burnout and Absenteeism: The stress from ineffective management can result in physical illness and burnout. When employees experience burnout and cannot attend work, it creates a ripple effect, adversely affecting those who must take on additional responsibilities.

• Low Productivity: When employees do not receive clear guidance or direction from their managers regarding priorities, they may feel overwhelmed and struggle to prioritize and complete their tasks effectively. Furthermore, a lack of professional growth opportunities can diminish their motivation to excel in their daily responsibilities.

Enhancing managerial effectiveness through one-on-one meetings is a valuable strategy. It is not surprising that many managers find these meetings to be very or extremely beneficial in supporting their direct reports; however, certain conditions must be met for direct reports to fully realize these benefits.

1.4 How can Managerial Effectiveness be improved?

Enhancing Managerial Effectiveness often necessitates a dedication to ongoing learning and professional development. Managers may engage in leadership training initiatives aimed at refining critical competencies such as communication, decision-making, problem-solving, strategic thinking, and emotional intelligence. Furthermore, actively seeking and responding to feedback from colleagues, supervisors, and team members is essential for identifying areas for improvement. Effective managers should also cultivate their capacity to adapt to change, given the ever-evolving nature of the business landscape. Finally, establishing robust relationships within their teams and fostering a culture of collaboration and mutual respect can significantly contribute to improved Managerial Effectiveness. Unsurprisingly, numerous managers consider their one-on-one meetings to be very or extremely beneficial in supporting their direct reports. However, these meetings must occur regularly and consistently for direct reports to fully realize the advantages.

More than 80% of employees who have weekly one-on-ones report receiving the necessary support from their managers during the pandemic, in contrast to only 66% of those with less frequent interactions. Whether conducted in person or through video conferencing, these meetings are instrumental in building trust, promoting accountability, supporting development, and actively reducing turnover. Employees who experience infrequent one-on-ones are at times more likely to indicate they are currently seeking new employment.

In comparison to those with less frequent discussions with their managers, employees who have at least weekly one-on-ones:

• Exhibit greater trust in senior leadership within their organization

• Feel more at ease discussing problems and challenging issues with their managers

• Are more often motivated to exceed their job responsibilities

• Experience greater inspiration from their work

• Have a clearer understanding of their contributions and how they align with the company's overarching objectives

High-quality one-on-ones allow leaders to engage with their employees throughout the week, allowing managers to gather crucial information for overall effectiveness.

1.5 What are the qualities of an effective manager?

A proficient manager embodies a diverse array of attributes. Essentially among these are strong communication skills, which are essential for effectively articulating goals, expectations, feedback, and decisions to team members. The capacity to inspire and motivate is equally vital for enhancing performance and fostering engagement within the team. Emotional intelligence, which includes self-awareness, empathy, and the ability to manage emotions, allows managers to navigate interpersonal dynamics with care and understanding. Effective problem-solving abilities, adaptability to change, and a results-oriented mindset are also indispensable.

Competent managers also excel in cultivating and sustaining robust relationships, delegating responsibilities judiciously, and offering constructive feedback. Exceptional managers significantly influence various aspects that contribute to organizational success, such as employee engagement, professional growth, productivity, and turnover rates. However, for managers to be truly effective, they require appropriate tools, structures, and practices—elements that many leaders currently lack. Current challenges faced by managers Manager are not only addressing their own challenges but are also guiding employees through theirs. This added responsibility is considerable and has resulted in managers feeling increasingly unprepared and more challenged than ever. Indeed, 65% of managers' report that they are finding it more difficult than usual to perform their roles effectively during the pandemic, with this figure rising to 76% among senior management. There are numerous factors contributing to the struggles faced by managers today, including personal, financial, or health-related issues. However, surveys identified certain primary concerns: The heightened stress due to global events In light of worldwide pandemics and armed conflicts, individuals are managing more responsibilities than ever, both professionally and personally. Managers are tasked with addressing their team members' emotional needs alongside their work requirements, yet they often lack the appropriate practices to do so effectively.

The attainment of team objectives serves as a clear indicator, as proficient managers guide their teams to meet established goals. Furthermore, employee satisfaction and engagement levels provide valuable insights into managerial performance, as effective management often cultivates a supportive and motivating workplace. The calibre of decision-making, encompassing the timeliness, relevance, and results of those decisions, is another significant measure. Additionally, feedback from team members and colleagues offers critical perspectives on a manager's effectiveness. Other relevant metrics may include employee turnover rates and the team's capacity to adapt and respond to changes under the manager's guidance. To make informed investments in managerial development, it is vital to first evaluate your managers' current effectiveness, identifying their strengths and areas for improvement.

Establishing baseline metrics is a fundamental step in formulating a strategic plan, and the implementation of continuous measurement and enhancement processes is equally essential.

1.6 Key Takeaways

The role of managers has historically been challenging, however, recent developments over the past few years have exacerbated these difficulties. Managerial Effectiveness pertains to the degree to which managers accomplish their intended outcomes within their groups/teams or departments. It encompasses individual's proficiency in establishing objectives. Competent managers play a crucial role in realizing business goals and objectives, as they coordinate efforts, guide team members, and ensure that tasks are executed effectively and efficiently. Managers may engage in leadership training initiatives aimed at refining critical competencies such as communication, decision-making, problem-solving, strategic thinking, and emotional intelligence.

Part 2: Learning Managerial Capabilities

2.1 What are Managerial Capabilities?

Managerial capabilities refer to the essential attributes or competencies that an executive must have to effectively carry out designated responsibilities within an organization. These skills encompass the ability to execute managerial functions while preventing crises and addressing issues swiftly as they arise. Such skills can be cultivated through both education and hands-on experience in a managerial role. They enable managers to engage effectively with colleagues and manage their subordinates adeptly, facilitating a smooth operational flow within the organization.

Recent taxonomies concerning global leadership competencies have indicated that the ability to learn is crucial for success in international positions. For instance, Kanter (1995) characterized an individual who can "learn from and utilize the diversity and unpredictability of the global marketplace." Additionally, Gregersen, Morrison, and Black (1998) identified inquisitiveness as a vital attribute of a successful international manager. Furthermore, Spreitzer, McCall, and Mahoney (1997) noted that individuals who actively seek learning opportunities, solicit and apply feedback, remain receptive to criticism, and exhibit flexibility and a willingness to engage across cultures are more likely to excel in international executive roles.

2.2 Importance of Competent Managers

Effective management skills are essential for the success of any organization in reaching its goals and objectives. A manager who cultivates strong management abilities can advance the company's mission and vision or business objectives with reduced obstacles and resistance from both internal and external stakeholders. Management and leadership skills are frequently synonymous, encompassing planning, decision-making, problem-solving, communication, delegation, and time management. Competent managers typically excel as leaders as well.

American social and organizational psychologist Robert Katz identifies three fundamental types of management skills:

1. **Technical Skills** Technical skills encompass the abilities and knowledge that enable managers to utilize various techniques to meet their goals. These skills include the operation of machinery, software, production tools, and equipment and the competencies required to enhance sales, design diverse products and services, and effectively market them.

2. **Conceptual Skills** Conceptual skills refer to the knowledge and ability of managers to engage in abstract thinking and idea formulation. A manager possessing these skills can comprehend an entire concept, analyse and diagnose issues, and devise innovative solutions. This capability allows the manager to anticipate potential challenges that their department or the organization may encounter.

3. **Human or Interpersonal Skills** Human or interpersonal skills reflect a manager's capacity to interact, collaborate, and relate effectively with individuals. These skills empower managers to leverage human potential within the organization and inspire employees to achieve improved outcomes.

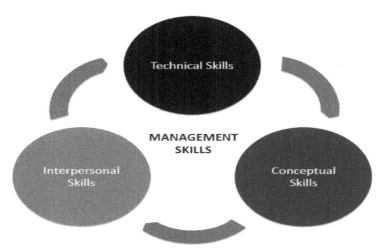

2.3 Management Skills Overview

Effective and efficient organizational management necessitates a diverse array of skills. Below are six fundamental management skills that every manager should possess to fulfil their responsibilities effectively:

1. Planning- Planning is an essential function within any organization. It encompasses the ability to structure activities according to established guidelines while adhering to the constraints of available resources, including time, finances, and personnel. This process involves devising a series of actions or strategies aimed at achieving specific goals or objectives with the resources at hand. The planning process entails identifying and establishing realistic goals, formulating necessary strategies, and detailing the tasks and timelines required to reach these objectives. Without a well-structured plan, achieving success becomes significantly more challenging.

2. Communication- Strong communication skills are imperative for a manager. They play a crucial role in effectively disseminating information within a team, fostering a cohesive working environment. The effectiveness of a manager's communication with their team directly influences

the adherence to established procedures, the completion of tasks, and ultimately, the organization's overall success. Communication encompasses the exchange of information within the organization, whether it is formal or informal, verbal or written, and can occur in various directions—vertical or horizontal. Clear communication channels enable managers to collaborate with their teams, mitigate conflicts, and address issues promptly. A manager adept in communication can build strong relationships with employees, facilitating the achievement of the organization's goals and objectives.

3. Decision-making- An essential skill in management is decision-making. Managers are faced with a multitude of decisions, whether consciously or unconsciously, and the ability to make sound decisions is crucial for a manager's effectiveness. The success of an organization often hinges on the quality of decisions made; sound decisions can lead to organizational success, whereas poor choices may result in failure or subpar performance. To ensure the organization operates efficiently, it is imperative that decisions are made with clarity and accuracy. A manager must take responsibility for each decision and be prepared to accept the consequences of those choices. Effective decision-making skills are vital for a manager, as they significantly influence the achievement of organizational goals.

4. Delegation- Delegation represents another fundamental management skill. It entails the process of assigning work-related tasks and responsibilities to other employees or subordinates. This process allows for the redistribution of tasks based on current workloads, enabling managers to allocate responsibilities effectively. A manager who excels in delegation can efficiently assign tasks and empower the appropriate employees with authority. When executed properly, delegation enhances the efficiency of task completion. Effective delegation enables managers to conserve time, maximize productivity, and foster a sense of responsibility and accountability among employees. It is essential for every manager to develop strong delegation skills to achieve optimal outcomes and meet productivity targets.

5. Problem-solving- Problem-solving constitutes a vital competency for effective management. A proficient manager must possess the capability to address and resolve the various challenges that may emerge during a typical workday. In the realm of management, problem-solving entails recognizing a specific issue or circumstance and subsequently determining the most effective approach to address it, thereby achieving an optimal resolution. This skill enables a manager to navigate complexities even when circumstances are less than ideal. A manager's strong problem-solving abilities sets them apart from their peers and instills confidence in their subordinates regarding their leadership capabilities.

6. Motivating- The capacity to motivate is a crucial skill within any organization. Motivation plays a significant role in eliciting desired behaviours or responses from employees and other stakeholders. Managers have access to various motivational strategies, and selecting appropriate methods often hinges on factors such as organizational culture, team dynamics, and individual personalities. There are two main categories of motivation that a manager can employ: intrinsic motivation, which arises from within the individual, and extrinsic motivation, which is influenced by external rewards.

2.4 Developing Personality & Self Awareness

Learning Behaviours. The learning capabilities integrated into a model which encompass self-development, perspective-taking, and cultural adaptability. In incorporating these learning capabilities and skills, the prime objective was to ascertain whether the learning behaviours linked to experiential or action learning would interact with global complexity to forecast managerial effectiveness. To this point experts aimed to investigate how individuals cultivate these learning skills. Are these learning skills associated with personality traits such as emotional stability (neuroticism) and openness to experience? Is the capacity to learn more closely related to personality, or do adult experiences of cultural diversity and early exposure to varied cultures provide a better explanation for this ability? Furthermore, can managers develop these learning behaviours? If learning skills correlate with effectiveness in a global context, and if these skills can be either trait-based or experience-based, we framed the process of preparing individuals for global managerial roles as a matter of selection, development, or a combination of both. Self-Development. Self-development refers to a collection of behaviours individuals would display if they took charge of their growth. It illustrates a proactive approach to personal development rather than a passive one. Characteristics of this learning orientation include a clear awareness of one's strengths and weaknesses, receptiveness to feedback regarding one's actions, and a willingness to pursue new experiences.

Perspective taking encompasses a range of skills and behaviors that characterize an individual who excels in active listening, considers various viewpoints, explores multiple potential solutions, and demonstrates empathy towards the perspectives of others. This concept may be regarded as one of the "personal intelligences" identified by Gardner (1983). In his work, Gardner (1983) identified six fundamental intelligences: (1) linguistic, (2) musical, (3) logical-mathematical, (4) spatial, (5) bodily-kinesthetic, and (6) personal.

Personal intelligence encompasses self-awareness (intrapersonal) and an understanding of others (interpersonal). Gardner distinguished these personal intelligences from the other five, positing that intrapersonal intelligence provides insight into one's own emotional experiences, while interpersonal intelligence involves the capacity to discern and differentiate among the emotions, temperaments, motivations, and intentions of others. He noted that personal intelligences are inherently more unique and less comparable, potentially even incomprehensible to individuals from different cultures. He stated, "the 'natural course' of the personal intelligence is more attenuated than that of other forms, as the specific symbolic and interpretive systems of each culture significantly influence these forms of information processing" (p. 240). Gardner's insights have implications for our discussion on perspective taking and cultural adaptability. These concepts represent the pinnacle of intrapersonal and interpersonal intelligences. An effective global manager ideally transcends their own cultural perceptions of self and others, effectively integrating their intrapersonal and interpersonal insights.

Cultural adaptability refers to a collection of behaviours exhibited by individuals who are driven to comprehend the impact of culture on behaviour and possess the ability to learn about and apply cultural distinctions. It extends beyond merely understanding a specific culture; it characterizes individuals who can effectively engage across various cultural contexts. This concept may be viewed as a specific instance of perspective-taking. Additionally, cultural adaptability may include the notion of cultural empathy, as identified by Ruben (1976) and further explored by Cui and Van Den Berg (1991). The idea of cultural adaptability is not new; it has its roots in the training literature associated with organizations such as the Peace Corps, religious missionary groups, the diplomatic service, the military, and the business sector. These entities have faced challenges in equipping individuals to operate successfully within diverse cultural environments.

2.5 Managerial Capabilities in a Nutshell

Management Capabilities encompass a range of competencies, including business planning, decision-making, problem-solving, effective communication, delegation, and time management. Although the specific skill sets required may vary across different roles and organizations, possessing strong management skills enables professionals to distinguish themselves and thrive at any level. In senior management positions, these skills are crucial for effectively leading an organization and attaining its strategic business goals.

2.6 Key Takeaways

Managerial capabilities refer to the essential attributes or competencies that an executive /manager must have to carry out designated responsibilities within an organization effectively. A manager who cultivates strong management abilities can advance the company's mission and vision or business objectives with reduced obstacles and resistance from both internal and external stakeholders. Management and leadership skills are frequently synonymous, encompassing planning, decision-making, problem-solving, communication, delegation, and time management. The learning capabilities integrated into a model which encompass self-development, perspective-taking, and cultural adaptability.

Part 3: Problem Solving & Building Better Work Culture

3.1 Problem Solving Skills

In purview both professional and personal contexts, challenges may turn up unexpectedly. Initially, one may be uncertain about how to address these issues; however, reflecting on the origins of the problem can provide clarity. Effective solutions can be identified or verified by maintaining composure and applying logical reasoning. This rational approach, characterized by a calm and creative mindset, is known as problem solving. It is an effective method for addressing various difficulties, ranging from navigating rumours in academic or corporate settings to determining appropriate actions when a crucial set-back may fail to find a feasible outcome at the workplace.

To fully understand and appreciate the significance of problem-solving skills in a professional environment and work sphere, it becomes essential to first comprehend the comprehensive skill set commonly associated with the term "problem-solving skills." In essence, problem-solving encompasses an individual's capacity to navigate and devise solutions for intricate and unforeseen circumstances effectively. Individuals who excel in problem-solving typically exhibit a blend of analytical and creative thinking abilities. They demonstrate a readiness to make decisions and possess the confidence to confront challenges within the workplace. Such individuals combine analytical, creative, and critical-thinking skills and a keen attention to detail. Consequently, they are adept at swiftly recognizing issues as they emerge and determining the most suitable solutions. Moreover, they can identify the underlying factors that may have contributed to the problem and initiate changes to prevent similar challenges in the future.

3.2 Why Problem-Solving Skills are Essential?

Life is inherently filled with problems and unpredictable situations, ranging from troubleshooting and figuring out a malfunctioning Computer System to managing a difficult customer in a professional setting. Employers in recent times are interested in understanding managers approach to problem-solving, as they seek individuals who view obstacles as opportunities for resolution through logical and effective strategies.

Individual must possess Effective Managerial traits for problem solving:

1. Listening Skills - Individuals who excel in active listening are typically adept at resolving issues. They attentively absorb information from their surroundings, which is crucial for addressing the challenges they face. Furthermore, they appreciate the significance of acknowledging the perspectives and experiences of others, which aids in understanding the root causes of problems and determining the most effective strategies for resolution.

2. Analytical Thinking Skills- Those who possess strong analytical thinking abilities can discern the underlying logical factors contributing to a problem, anticipate the potential long-term consequences, and evaluate the effectiveness of various solutions to identify the most viable option. Consequently, evaluating analytical thinking capabilities during the hiring process is imperative.

3. Creative Thinking Skills -Creative thinkers are capable of integrating their analytical abilities with innovative approaches to tackle challenges. This skill set allows individuals to discover novel and forward-thinking solutions to various issues. As a result, they can offer fresh insights and propose imaginative and experimental strategies to address a wide range of problems.

4. Coordinating Skills- Effective problem solvers must also demonstrate strong coordination skills. The capacity to convey and operate complex information clearly and concisely is a significant advantage for employers operating in dynamic environments.

5. Decision-Making Skills- Individuals equipped with problem-solving skills are also proficient in making decisions and exhibiting confidence in their choices. This capability is crucial, as effective problem-solving often necessitates making definitive decisions to achieve successful outcomes.

6. Teamwork- While independent thinking is essential for problem solvers, the ability to collaborate effectively within a group or team is equally important. Arriving at the optimal solution frequently requires collective effort, making it vital for candidates to showcase their ability to inspire others to generate the best solutions and work collaboratively in developing and implementing those solutions.

3.3 Building Problem-Solving Skills at Work

When encountering a problems in the workplace, manager may consider applying the following five-step approach to determine towards a resolution to retain achievable outcome:

1. Articulate the issue and formulate a clear 'problem statement'.

2. Assess the current situation to discern what aspects are functioning well and which are not.

3. Pinpoint the potential origins of the issue.

4. Determine the most likely cause and conduct a test to verify it.

5. Implement measures to resolve the issue.

Reflecting on past experiences, manager may have successfully navigated challenges and taken pride in your contributions. It is beneficial to analyze what strategies were effective and which were less so. Enhancing problem-solving abilities in the workplace and everyday life will enable any individual to assess their situations and information, breaking them down into manageable components. Reframe challenges as opportunities for solutions rather than insurmountable obstacles. Strengthen their decision-making capabilities by relying on data and logic rather than solely on intuition. Uncover personal strengths and skills that they may not have previously recognized. Experience personal growth and learning with each challenge that individual successfully navigate. Demonstrate to potential employers that the manager possesses practical, creative, and adaptable qualities, making them a dependable asset.

3.4 Tools of Problem-Solving Skills

Recommendations by experts have the following tools to assist managers in identifying the problem and analyzing its causes, including the prime cause:

The 5W's (along with the 5 WHY's)

The 5W's methodology is particularly effective in problem definition and subsequent assessment of whether additional data or analysis is necessary. To define a problem, one can consider the following aspects:

WHAT: Identify the characteristics of the problem—what exactly is the issue? Subsequently, pose questions such as, "What information do I require? What would be the ideal outcome? What metrics shall we employ to determine if the problem has been resolved?" It is also beneficial to ask the 'what' question multiple times to delve deeper. For instance, if a 'what' inquiry reveals skill shortages as a concern, one should then inquire, "What specific skills are lacking?" If the response is "communication skills," the next question would be, "What particular communication skills are needed?"

WHERE: Determine the structural or physical location of the problem. Where does the issue typically arise? Additionally, where might we anticipate potential challenges?

WHEN: Assess the timing of the problem. When does it occur? When is it imperative to address the issue? When will we implement a solution?

WHO: Identify the individuals impacted by the problem. Who is responsible for the issue? Who are the key stakeholders involved, including customers, partners, and employees? Who will make the determination regarding the resolution of the problem?

WHY: Explore the reasons behind the necessity to resolve the problem. Why is this situation occurring? Why are individuals responding in specific ways? The 'why' question aims to uncover the fundamental causes and contributing factors of the problem. It is common to ask the 'why' question five times to thoroughly investigate and identify root causes, a technique known as the 5 WHY's, which serves as a method for root cause analysis. The objective is to identify the underlying causes of the problem rather than merely addressing its symptoms.

Johari Window

Enhancing self-awareness and personal development within group settings is essential for individuals. The 'Johari' window model serves as an effective tool for fostering understanding and improving communication among group members. Developed in 1955 by American psychologists Joseph Luft and Harry Ingham, this model emerged from their research on group dynamics at the University of California and was subsequently refined by Luft. The term 'Johari' is a combination of the first names of its creators. This model is also referred to as the feedback/disclosure model of self-awareness.

The Johari window model serves to improve an individual's understanding of others. This framework is founded on two key principles: trust can be built by disclosing personal information to others, and self-awareness can be gained through their feedback. In the Johari model, each individual is depicted through four quadrants or panes, each representing personal information, emotions, motivations, and the degree to which this information is known or unknown to oneself or others from four different perspectives.

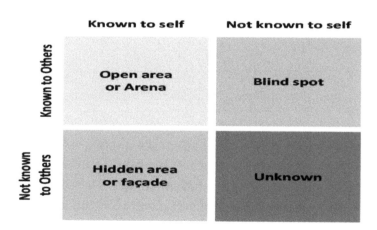

1. **Open/Self-Area or Arena** – This domain encompasses the individual's personal information, including their attitudes, behaviors, emotions, feelings, skills, and perspectives, which both the individual and others recognize. It serves as the primary space for communication; as this arena expands, the relationships within it become increasingly effective and dynamic. The 'feedback solicitation' process involves actively seeking and listening to feedback from others, which can help broaden the open area while minimizing the blind spot. Additionally, the arena can be

expanded downward by disclosing personal feelings, thereby reducing the hidden and unknown areas.

2. **Blind Self or Blind Spot** – This refers to aspects of yourself that are known to others within a group but remain unknown to you. Others may perceive you in ways that differ from your own self-perception. To enhance communication efficiency, it is essential to minimize the blind spot by actively seeking feedback from those around you.

3. **Hidden Area or Façade** – This area contains information that you are aware of but choose to keep from others. Such information may include personal feelings, past experiences, fears, and secrets that you prefer to keep private, as they can influence relationships. To foster healthier interactions, reducing the hidden area by sharing relevant information and moving it into the open area is important.

4. **Unknown Area** – This domain consists of information, feelings, abilities, and talents not recognized by yourself or others. Such unawareness may stem from past traumatic experiences or events that remain undiscovered throughout one's life. Individuals may only become aware of their hidden qualities and capabilities through self-discovery or by observing others. Open communication is a valuable strategy for diminishing the unknown area, facilitating more effective interactions.

Mind Mapping & Brainstorming

Mind mapping serves as a powerful tool for brainstorming and organizing thoughts. A mind map is a visual representation that systematically arranges information, beginning with a central theme or concept and branching out to encompass new and related ideas that extend from the core. By concentrating on essential concepts articulated in your own language and exploring the relationships among them, you can effectively chart knowledge to enhance your comprehension and retention of information.

Brainstorming is widely recognized as an effective collaborative approach to problem-solving. A review of various definitions indicates that it is generally characterized as a method for: - Conducting group discussions to gather all ideas - Encouraging innovative thought processes - Fostering unplanned contributions from participants - Addressing specific questions or challenges through collective problem-solving - Producing novel ideas or creative solutions by employing lateral thinking techniques - Capturing all suggestions without immediate criticism or evaluation, reserving such analysis for a later stage.

Affinity Mapping

Once the preliminary research on a subject is located or verified, affinity mapping serves as an effective method for visualizing and organizing that information. This approach allows for a dynamic recording of qualitative and quantitative data gathered from on-site observations and interviews. The initial phase of affinity mapping requires manager to write their findings on individual sticky notes, which are then organized into groups based on relevant topics (for instance, business trends, challenges at work, and motivational themes) and subsequently categorized under appropriate headings. It is important to remain flexible, as the process of affinity mapping is inherently dynamic, allowing for the rearrangement of sticky notes as needed.

3.5 Problem-Solving Skills Advantages

Problem-solving skills offer numerous significant advantages in the workplace. Let us explore on the most crucial benefits that effective problem solvers contribute to their roles and organizations:

- Proficiency in intelligent time management-Time management is often an overlooked aspect of problem-solving skills in professional settings. However, individuals with strong problem-solving capabilities typically exhibit exceptional time management skills. Their ability to allocate time effectively and concentrate on critical business priorities enhances decision-making and positively influences business outcomes.

- Competence in prioritizing, planning, and executing strategies -Individuals skilled in problem-solving excel at thoroughly evaluating customer and organizational needs, allowing them to prioritize, plan, and implement strategies effectively. They are adept at managing various components and devising strategies to address multiple distinct demands.

- Capacity for innovative thinking- Problem solvers frequently uncover hidden opportunities within challenges. The ability to think creatively is a vital problem-solving skill in the workplace, as it can lead to outcomes that surpass initial expectations.

- Capability to perform under pressure This is often regarded as one of the most critical advantages of problem-solving skills in a professional environment. Problem solvers tend to thrive under pressure, particularly when faced with tight deadlines and evolving project requirements. Depending on the organizational culture, there may be a preference for individuals who can provide rapid solutions or those who take a more measured approach to identify subsequent steps. Both approaches are valuable and essential qualities in problem-solving.

- Skill in risk management Effective planning is a key component of problem-solving. Problem solvers are equipped to tackle immediate issues and possess the foresight to anticipate future challenges based on trends, patterns, experiences, and current events.

3.6 Key Takeaways

Problem Solving demonstrates a readiness to make decisions and the confidence to confront challenges within the workplace. Such individuals combine analytical, creative, and critical-thinking skills and a keen attention to detail. Consequently, they are adept at swiftly recognizing issues as they emerge and determining the most suitable solutions. Employers in recent times are interested in understanding managers approach to problem-solving, as they seek individuals who view obstacles as opportunities for resolution through logical and effective strategies.

Part 4: Interpersonal & Group Behaviour

4.1 Interpersonal Behaviour

Interpersonal behaviour encompasses the actions and interactions that occur within human relationships. It includes the various ways individuals communicate, which can be classified as interpersonal behaviour. This behaviour may manifest through both verbal communication and nonverbal signals, such as body language and facial expressions. Verbal interpersonal behaviour can involve humour, storytelling, and the exchange of directives. Proficient interpersonal skills are highly valued in numerous contexts, particularly in professions that depend on personal interactions, such as healthcare and sales. Interpersonal behaviour refers to the dynamics between two individuals in any environment. It is crucial in organizations, educational institutions, and other settings to foster strong interpersonal relationships. When the relationship between two individuals is robust and positive, it promotes appropriate behaviour, leading to productive outcomes, which organizations strive to achieve. At the managerial level, the presence of trust and enthusiasm for work can foster unity, resulting in significant achievements.

4.2 Group Behaviour

When individuals collaborate to function together, they create a collective known as a group. They engage in dialogue and depend on each other. Their interests align, and they work towards common objectives. Understanding group dynamics is essential for grasping organizational behaviour. This concept encompasses the interactions and influences that occur among members within a social context.

Definition

Stephen P. Robbins defines a group as "two or more individuals who interact and are interdependent, united to achieve specific goals." Arnold and Feldman describe a work group as "a collection of two or more individuals who engage with one another, share similar interests, and collaborate to complete a work-related task." Official Group: This type of group is structured by the organization and is established with formal approval. It is based on designated roles and responsibilities, with tasks assigned to be completed. Such groups tend to be more permanent, and members are expected to follow established policies and procedures. Unofficial Group (Clique): This group is not formally organized or predetermined. It emerges naturally within the workplace without management's endorsement. Members of this group share common interests and seek social interaction. Participation is voluntary, and individuals may belong to multiple unofficial groups, with personal relationships being the primary focus.

4.3 Group Structure & Cohesiveness

Each group is structured in a specific manner. The organization of the group significantly influences the behaviour of its members and affects the dynamics within the group. Factors associated with group organization are considered independent and flexible by nature. Roles Norms Status Group

Cohesiveness Status refers to a rank assigned to individuals or groups by societal consensus. It is essential for understanding behaviour, as it encompasses the significant behavioural effects of status symbols and the equity of status.

Examples of status symbols include titles, company vehicles, personal assistants, reserved parking spaces, and memberships in exclusive organizations. The equity of status is vital for group dynamics. Members must perceive the status hierarchy as just; otherwise, status inequality leads to imbalance. Typically, groups can establish criteria for ranking among their members. Examples of status include: Attending a prestigious university Living in an affluent area Being part of exclusive clubs Rights associated with executive positions Owning a luxury vehicle Associating with reputable companies.

Group Cohesiveness The level of cohesiveness within a group can vary. Cohesion refers to members' degree of attraction and motivation to remain united. Sources of Cohesive Groups These include: Interaction: Regular interactions among members enhance group cohesion. Threat: External threats can strengthen group cohesion by bringing members together. Entry: Groups that are more challenging to join tend to exhibit greater cohesion. Collaboration: A cooperative atmosphere within the group bolsters cohesiveness. Common Objectives: Shared goals enhance the unity of the group. Attitudes and Values: Cohesion is strengthened by common attitudes and values among members, providing social validation for their beliefs. Group Size: Smaller groups tend to promote cohesion, while larger groups can hinder communication, create conflict and dissatisfaction, and limit opportunities for connection.

4.4 Stages of Development

The process by which individuals learn to collaborate effectively is referred to as team development. Studies indicate that teams typically progress through specific stages during this development. Bruce Tuckman, an educational psychologist, delineated a five-stage process that most teams undergo to achieve high performance.

1. **The forming stage** represents an initial phase characterized by orientation and familiarization among team members. During this period, uncertainty prevails, prompting individuals to seek guidance and leadership. A member who demonstrates authority or possesses expertise may be perceived as a potential leader. Team members often contemplate questions such as, "What benefits does the team provide me?" "What are my responsibilities?" and "Will I be accepted?" Most interactions during this stage are social, as individuals strive to establish connections with one another.

2. **The storming stage** is recognized as the most challenging and pivotal phase in team development. This period is characterized by conflict and competition as distinct personalities begin to surface. Team performance may decline during this stage, as energy is diverted towards unproductive endeavors. Disagreements regarding team objectives may arise, forming subgroups and cliques around dominant personalities or shared viewpoints. To navigate this stage successfully, team members must confront challenges, embrace individual differences, and reconcile conflicting perspectives on tasks and goals. If unresolved, conflicts can hinder progress and create enduring issues.

3. **The norming stage** Upon successfully navigating the storming stage, teams enter the norming stage, where conflicts are resolved and a sense of unity begins to take shape. During this phase, consensus emerges regarding leadership roles and the responsibilities of individual members. Interpersonal differences are addressed, fostering a sense of cohesion and collaboration. As team members learn to work together effectively, overall performance improves. However, this harmony remains fragile; the team risks regressing to the storming stage if disagreements resurface.

4. **The performing stage** signifies a mature and well-organized team with firmly established consensus and collaboration. A clear and stable structure is in place, and members are dedicated to the team's objectives. Although challenges and conflicts may still arise, they are managed in a constructive manner. The dynamics of conflict and its resolution will be further explored in subsequent discussions.

5. **The adjourning stage**, the majority of the team's objectives have been successfully met. The focus shifts towards completing remaining tasks and recording the efforts and outcomes achieved. As the workload decreases, individual members may be reassigned to different teams, leading to the original group's disbandment. This transition may evoke feelings of regret as the team concludes its work; therefore, a formal recognition of the team's achievements can be beneficial. In cases where the team functions as a standing committee with ongoing responsibilities, new members may be introduced, prompting the team to revert to either the forming or storming stages and undergo the development process anew.

4.5 Team Building

How did the manager determine the appropriate way to behave when participating in a team? What indicators informed the manager about acceptable conduct or the expected level of performance? Typically, teams establish norms that direct the actions of their members. These norms create a benchmark for behaviour, attitude, and performance that all members are anticipated to adhere to. While norms resemble rules, they are not formally documented but are understood implicitly by all team members. Their effectiveness stems from the desire of team members to support one another and maintain harmonious relationships, with peer pressure or sanctions in place to ensure adherence when norms are breached. Norm formation arises from team members' interactions throughout the developmental stages. In the initial forming and storming phases, norms primarily address expectations regarding attendance and commitment. As the team progresses into the norming and performing stages, the focus shifts to interpersonal relationships and performance levels. Performance norms are particularly crucial as they delineate the effort and standards necessary for the team's success. It is important to note that leaders play a significant role in cultivating effective norms by serving as role models and recognizing desired behaviours. For norms to effectively regulate behaviour, they must be embraced by the team members. The degree of cohesiveness within the team largely influences whether members accept and adhere to these norms. Team cohesiveness refers to the extent to which members feel attracted to the team and are motivated to remain part of it. Members of highly cohesive teams appreciate their membership, are dedicated to team endeavors, and derive satisfaction from collective achievements. They strive to conform to norms to preserve their relationships and fulfill team expectations. Teams characterized by robust performance norms and high levels of cohesiveness tend to achieve superior performance outcomes.

4.6 Key Takeaways

Interpersonal behaviour refers to the dynamics between two individuals in any environment. It is crucial in organizations, educational institutions, and other settings to foster strong interpersonal relationships. Each group is structured in a specific manner. The organization of the group significantly influences the behaviour of its members and affects the dynamics within the group. How did the manager determine the appropriate way to behave when participating in a team? What indicators informed the manager about acceptable conduct or the expected level of performance? Typically, teams establish norms that direct the actions of their members. These norms create a benchmark for behaviour, attitude, and performance that all members are anticipated to follow through.

Part 5: Role Of Global Managers

5.1 What Global Managers Do?

Global can be termed as worldwide hence, global managers and executives has a crucial role to play for the development of businesses and organisations for economic growth. Learned expert examined and emphasized the significance of the characteristics of liaison (networking across organizational boundaries) and spokesperson managers execute regularly. This indicates that as responsibilities transition from domestic to global contexts, managers increasingly prioritize external roles at the organization's periphery. Furthermore, global managers are required to sustain the managerial skills of cultural adaptability, international business acumen, and time management as more critical to their roles compared to local managers. These findings by behavioural scientists and educationists align with our definition of a global manager—one who oversees and leads across distances, borders, and cultural expectations. An interesting finding that merits further exploration is that the roles and skills deemed most essential by global managers—liaison, spokesperson, and time management—differed from those recognized by their superiors as vital for managerial effectiveness.

Global managers serve as the essential connection between a company's competencies and the demands of the international market. They are tasked with operating locally within their home country while maintaining a global perspective. This necessitates a deep understanding of their cultural context and an openness to embracing diverse foreign cultures. A global manager functions as a unifying force within their organization. This type of manager can grasp the organization's internal dynamics while remaining attuned to global challenges such as cultural diversity. They are adept at navigating differences in people, values, and cultures, and they effectively communicate this awareness to their teams.

5.2 Scope of Global Managers

The characteristics, role competencies, and abilities required for global managers to perform effectively bear a resemblance to those needed by local managers. Supervisors of global managers emphasize that emotional stability, proficiency in leadership and decision-making roles, and the capacity to manage stress are key elements of managerial effectiveness, irrespective of the complexities associated with global responsibilities. Furthermore, supervisors value traits such as conscientiousness, expertise in negotiation and innovation, business acumen, knowledge of international business, cultural adaptability, and the ability to understand diverse perspectives as pivotal acumen for the success of global managers. Emotional stability becomes particularly significant when examining the relationship between personality traits and managerial effectiveness. It seems that the roles of decision-maker and negotiator are more vital for global managers compared to their domestic counterparts. Additionally, the ability to learn effectively is deemed considerably more important for the performance evaluations of global managers. While these factors may align with common expectations, it is somewhat unexpected that conscientiousness and business knowledge did not show a significant correlation with the effectiveness ratings of domestic managers.

The correlation between experience and effectiveness fetched results that largely contradicts business uncertainties. Factors such as early exposure to diverse languages and cultures, living abroad, workplace multilingualism, and previous involvement with diverse teams did not serve as reliable predictors of effectiveness ratings in either global or domestic settings. Notably, managers who embodied a highly cosmopolitan profile—characterized by multilingualism and extensive travel—may not necessarily receive good ratings from their superiors regarding their likability and trustworthiness among peers and colleagues within their organizations. This outcome may highlight a paradoxical aspect for managers perceived as cosmopolitan: while exposure to various cultures through education, expatriate assignments, language acquisition, and travel is essential for cultivating the competencies required for effective global management, these same experiences are linked to unfavorable evaluations from superiors in at least one dimension of effectiveness.

Bennett's (1993) research on the implications of marginality sheds light on this paradox. Her findings illustrated how certain individuals cultivate an identity that transcends cultural boundaries as a result of extensive exposure to various cultures. This cultural autonomy allows them to navigate between different cultural contexts more effectively; however, it simultaneously creates a barrier in their interpersonal relationships and influences perceptions of their effectiveness. Therefore it can be reflected on examination of cohort homogeneity as a variable factor in experience, which aimed to evaluate the fact that a supervisor's assessment of an individual's effectiveness could be swayed by the degree of similarity between that individual and other senior managers, particularly regarding demographics such as age, country of origin, tenure with the company, education, race, and gender. Three out of the four organizations studied in India observed modest cohort effects, albeit not in the anticipated direction. These findings imply that differences in education, nationality, gender, and tenure may shape supervisors' views on effectiveness until proper evaluation methodologies are obtained.

5.3 Need for Effective Global Managers

The contemporary dynamic and international landscape offers an ideal setting for leaders to investigate and master contemporary tools. It is essential that all our actions are viewed through a global perspective, as this global mindset is increasingly vital for today's managers.

In order to align with the highly globalized and ever-evolving world of today, experts have proposed that the leadership model that dominated the 20th century must be transformed to adopt a new approach to thinking, perceiving, decision-making, and existence. Organizations are required to make substantial investments in training and developing their personnel to meet the demands of global business, foster a culture of continuous learning among their workforce, and provide the necessary resources and tools to ensure that employees remain informed about emerging market dynamics and challenges.

It is essential for every organization to broaden its reach and participate in international platform. To succeed in these global markets, companies require highly skilled managers who possess a global mindset. This mindset is crucial for enabling managers to motivate individuals from diverse cultural backgrounds, political ideologies, institutional frameworks, and other contextual factors that affect their perceptions, attitude and behaviour, communication methods, and cognitive processes. Developing a global mindset necessitates healthy management practice. Leaders should create business and personal standards that are not confined to a single cultural viewpoint. A manager with a global outlook can perceive and anticipate situations that may elude other managers. By adopting a holistic approach, managers with global perspectives can identify opportunities and assess risks, thereby aligning their objectives with those of their organizations.

As a global manager, it is essential to recognize the significance of evaluating risk factors prior to embarking on new projects. Individual should possess the expertise and capability to develop a detailed plan and facilitate its execution. It is crucial to appreciate the importance of exploring various market options, conducting thorough analyses, and selecting the most effective strategy based on their findings. In addition to these essential competencies, there are several professional skills that competent manager must cultivate to become a prominent global manager:

• Assess the feasibility of foreign trade. need to balance potential advantages against possible risks to evaluate a market's viability. When initiating or expanding an international trade initiative, your expertise should guide you in determining whether a proposal will enhance revenue and align with your corporate objectives. Strategize for market expansion, formulate a comprehensive global business plan, and assist in its execution.

• Develop effective market entry strategies. Global managers understand the importance of researching and assessing potential market entry strategies and strategic partnerships before making informed decisions.

• Tailor products and services. It is imperative to recognize the critical importance of customizing products and services for specific international markets.

• Evaluate global marketing and sales. Manager must acknowledge that while marketing can stimulate demand, a robust sales strategy is necessary to leverage this interest effectively.

- Maintain cultural sensitivity. Manager should be cognizant of multicultural differences and their implications for global trade

- Adhere to global ethics and legal standards. It is vital to comply with all local and international legal regulations governing international commerce and to be well-versed in the fundamental legal principles of global business.

5.4 Key Takeaways

A global manager oversees the company's operations and projects internationally, while also formulating marketing campaigns and promotional strategies to enhance brand visibility, attract prospective clients, and boost revenue and profitability. This role involves monitoring the distribution process and product development, collaborating with various teams to implement campaign strategies, and analyzing prevailing market trends to uncover business opportunities that align with consumer needs and public interests. Additionally, a global manager manages the budget for international promotions, ensuring sufficient resources and materials are allocated to facilitate seamless operations.

Glossary of Key Terms in Fundamentals Of Managerial Effectiveness:

I. Managerial Effectiveness: The ability of a manager to achieve organizational goals efficiently and effectively by making the best use of resources, time, and people.

II. Leadership: The process of influencing and guiding individuals or groups to achieve common goals, while fostering motivation and commitment within the team.

III. Communication: The exchange of information, ideas, and feedback between individuals or groups within the organization, essential for coordination and decision-making.

IV. Delegation: The process of assigning responsibility and authority to subordinates to complete tasks, allowing managers to focus on higher-level strategic activities.

V. Decision-Making: The process of selecting the best course of action among alternatives to achieve desired outcomes.

VI. Motivation: The internal and external factors that stimulate individuals to take action towards achieving goals, crucial for driving performance and productivity.

VII. Goal Setting: The practice of defining clear, measurable, and time-bound objectives to guide the actions of employees and the organization.

VIII. Time Management: The ability to plan and organize tasks effectively to make the best use of available time, improving productivity and efficiency.

IX. Conflict Resolution: The methods and processes used to address and resolve disagreements or disputes within teams or between individuals in a way that fosters positive outcomes.

X. Team Building: The process of creating and developing effective teams by fostering collaboration, trust, and communication among team members.

Chapter 2: Managing Diversity, Equity and Inclusion

Part 1: Introduction

1.1. Definition of Diversity, Equity, and Inclusion (DEI)

Diversity refers to the presence of differences within a given setting. In the workplace, this includes differences in race, ethnicity, gender, age, sexual orientation, physical abilities, religion, socioeconomic status, and other identity characteristics. Diversity acknowledges that everyone brings a unique perspective and set of experiences that can enrich an organization.

Equity involves creating fair opportunities for all employees by recognizing and addressing systemic barriers and biases. Unlike equality, which treats everyone equally, equity is about ensuring everyone has access to the same opportunities and resources, accounting for individual needs and circumstances.

Inclusion is the practice of creating an environment where all individuals feel valued, respected, and able to contribute fully. Inclusion goes beyond simply having diverse groups within an organization; it involves active efforts to engage everyone, ensuring that diverse voices are heard and respected in decisionmaking processes.

1.2. Importance of DEI in Today's Business Landscape

In today's globalized and interconnected world, Diversity, Equity, and Inclusion (DEI) have become critical to organizational success. Here's why:

1. Enhanced Innovation and Creativity: Diverse teams bring together a wide range of perspectives, experiences, and ideas, leading to more creative problemsolving and innovation. When employees feel included and valued, they are more likely to contribute new ideas and challenge the status quo, driving the organization forward.

2. Improved Employee Engagement and Retention: An inclusive workplace where all employees feel respected and valued fosters higher levels of engagement and job satisfaction. When employees see that their organization is committed to DEI, they are more likely to stay with the company, reducing turnover and the associated costs.

3. Better DecisionMaking: Research shows that diverse teams are more likely to make better decisions because they consider a wider range of perspectives and avoid groupthink. This leads to more thorough analysis and more effective solutions.

4. Attracting Top Talent: Today's workforce, particularly younger generations, values diversity and inclusion. Companies that are seen as inclusive are more attractive to top talent, helping them to recruit the best and brightest from a broad talent pool.

5. Market Competitiveness: Companies that understand and reflect the diversity of their customer base are better positioned to serve those customers. By embracing DEI, organizations can better understand and meet the needs of diverse markets, leading to greater market share and customer loyalty.

6. Legal and Ethical Imperatives: In many regions, there are legal requirements related to antidiscrimination and equal opportunity in the workplace. Beyond compliance, companies have an ethical responsibility to ensure fair treatment for all employees, contributing to a just and equitable society.

7. Corporate Reputation and Brand Value: Companies that are known for their commitment to DEI often enjoy a stronger reputation, which can translate into greater customer loyalty, increased investor interest, and positive media attention. Conversely, failing to address DEI can result in reputational damage, particularly in the age of social media.

Thus, DEI is not just a trend or a moral imperative—it's a business necessity. Organizations that prioritize DEI are better equipped to thrive in today's complex and diverse business environment. By embracing and embedding DEI into their strategic HR practices, companies can unlock the full potential of their workforce, drive innovation, and achieve sustainable success.

1.3. Benefits of DEI

Diversity, Equity, and Inclusion (DEI) are not just ethical imperatives; they are powerful drivers of business success. The benefits of DEI extend across various aspects of an organization, leading to innovation, better decision making, and improved financial performance. Here's a closer look at these benefits:

Diverse Perspectives Lead To:

1. Innovation

The Power of Diversity in Creativity: Diverse teams bring a wide array of perspectives, experiences, and problem solving approaches. When individuals from different backgrounds collaborate, they combine their unique viewpoints, leading to creative solutions that may not emerge in homogeneous teams.

Example: A diverse team at a technology company might draw on different cultural experiences and user needs to develop a product that appeals to a broader market. This cross pollination of ideas often results in breakthrough innovations that can differentiate a company in a competitive market.

2. Better Decision Making

Avoiding Group think: Group think occurs when a homogeneous group of people makes decisions without critically evaluating alternative viewpoints. Diverse teams are less susceptible to group think because they naturally consider a wider range of perspectives and challenge each other's assumptions.

Comprehensive Analysis: When team members bring varied perspectives, they are more likely to explore different angles of a problem, consider potential risks, and develop more robust solutions. This comprehensive analysis leads to better decisions that take into account the needs and concerns of a broader audience.

3. Improved Financial Performance

Correlation Between Diversity and Profitability: Numerous studies have shown a strong correlation between diversity and financial performance. Companies with diverse leadership teams are more likely to outperform their peers. This is because diverse teams can better understand and serve diverse customer bases, leading to increased market share and revenue.

Example: A McKinsey study found that companies in the top quartile for gender diversity were 25% more likely to have aboveaverage profitability than companies in the bottom quartile. Similarly, companies with ethnic diversity at the executive level were 36% more likely to outperform their peers.

1.4. Examples of Companies That Have Benefited from DEI

1. Case Study: Google's Diverse Innovation Teams

Innovation through Diversity: Google has long been an advocate of diversity and inclusion, acknowledging that varied teams foster innovation. The company's dedication to constructing diverse teams has resulted in the creation of products that cater to a global audience. For instance, Google's Voice product accommodates a wide array of languages and accents, mirroring the diverse backgrounds of the engineers who contributed to its development.

Results: Google's emphasis on diversity has not only propelled product innovation but also bolstered its position as a global tech frontrunner with a robust, inclusive culture that attracts top talent worldwide.

2. Case Study: Johnson & Johnson's DEI Strategy

DEI as a Business Strategy: Johnson & Johnson (J&J) has ingrained DEI into its fundamental business strategy. The company's focus on assembling diverse teams and nurturing an inclusive environment has been pivotal in its triumph. J&J's DEI initiatives encompass leadership development programs for underrepresented groups and employee resource groups (ERGs) that advocate for diversity in the workplace.

Results: These endeavors have led to heightened employee engagement, elevated retention rates, and enhanced financial performance. Indeed, J&J has been heralded as a diversity trailblazer by numerous entities and has witnessed consistent growth in revenue and market share.

3. **Case Study: Microsoft's Inclusive Culture**

Leveraging Inclusion for Business Growth: Microsoft has made substantial progress in fostering an inclusive culture where all employees feel esteemed and empowered to contribute. The company's DEI endeavors encompass accessibility initiatives, endorsement of diverse hiring practices, and a focus on inclusive product design.

Results: Microsoft's unwavering commitment to DEI has given rise to the development of products that are more accessible and userfriendly, aiding the company in reaching a broader audience. The company's inclusive culture has also bolstered its standing as a preferred employer, attracting a diverse pool of talent and propelling business expansion.

The benefits of DEI are clear: embracing diversity, equity, and inclusion leads to innovation, better decisions, and stronger financial performance. Leading companies like Google, Johnson & Johnson, and Microsoft show that DEI is critical for a winning business strategy. Organizations prioritizing DEI will thrive in a diverse and dynamic global market.

1.5. Competitive Advantage: Attracting Top Talent, Enhancing Employee Engagement, and Improving Company Reputation

Diversity, Equity, and Inclusion have become increasingly important for organizations seeking to gain a competitive edge in today's global marketplace. A strong DEI strategy can offer numerous benefits, from attracting top talent to enhancing employee engagement and improving company reputation.

One of the primary advantages of a robust DEI strategy is its ability to attract and retain top talent. In an era of globalization, where the workforce is becoming increasingly diverse, employees are seeking companies that not only value diversity but actively foster an inclusive culture. As Gilbert et al. noted, "achieving an attractive image in the business world is eyecatching for new potential workers and one of the most important competitive advantages that allows for acquisition of unique human resources" (Kharroubi, 2020). When organizations demonstrate a genuine commitment to DEI, they are more likely to appeal to a wider pool of qualified candidates, including those from underrepresented groups.

Moreover, a diverse and inclusive workforce can lead to enhanced employee engagement. As the source indicates, "trust climate" and the relationship with the company are stronger when employees feel a sense of belonging and inclusion in the workplace. (Rahman, 2019) This, in turn, can contribute to increased productivity, creativity, and problemsolving abilities, all of which are crucial for maintaining a competitive edge.

Furthermore, a strong DEI strategy contributes significantly to improving a company's reputation. In today's socially conscious environment, consumers, investors, and other stakeholders are increasingly scrutinizing companies based on their commitment to social responsibility, which includes DEI efforts. Companies that are perceived as leaders in diversity and inclusion are often viewed more favorably by the public, which can translate into increased brand loyalty, customer satisfaction, and even financial performance.

As organizations demonstrate their commitment to DEI through transparent policies, practices, and results, they build trust and credibility with both internal and external stakeholders. This trust is not only crucial for attracting and retaining top talent but also for fostering longterm business relationships and gaining a competitive advantage in the market.

In addition, a wellexecuted DEI strategy can drive innovation by bringing together diverse perspectives and experiences. When employees from varied backgrounds collaborate, they are more likely to generate novel ideas and approaches, leading to innovative solutions that can differentiate the company from its competitors. This diversity of thought is a critical asset in today's fastpaced and everchanging business landscape.

In conclusion, a strong DEI strategy is not just a moral or ethical imperative; it is a strategic business advantage. By attracting top talent, enhancing employee engagement, and improving company reputation, organizations can position themselves as leaders in their industries, driving longterm success and sustainability. As the global marketplace continues to evolve, the importance of DEI will only grow, making it an essential component of any forwardthinking organization's strategy.

1.6. Risk Mitigation in Diversity, Equity, and Inclusion (DEI)

In the rapidly evolving landscape of modern business, Diversity, Equity, and Inclusion (DEI) have emerged as not only moral imperatives but also critical components of risk management. As organizations navigate an increasingly global and interconnected marketplace, the failure to effectively address DEI can lead to significant legal and ethical challenges. This chapter explores the risks associated with neglecting DEI, emphasizing the potential consequences for businesses and the importance of proactive risk mitigation strategies.

1.6.1 Legal Risks: The Threat of Discrimination Lawsuits and Regulatory Compliance

One of the most immediate and tangible risks of failing to prioritize Diversity, Equity, and Inclusion (DEI) is the potential for legal repercussions, particularly in the form of discrimination lawsuits. In an era where social justice movements and legal standards are driving increased scrutiny of workplace practices, businesses that do not actively foster an inclusive environment are at a heightened risk of legal action. Discrimination lawsuits can arise from various factors, including race, gender, sexual orientation, age, disability, and more.

These lawsuits often carry substantial financial burdens. Legal fees, settlements, and damages can quickly escalate, sometimes reaching millions of dollars. Beyond the immediate financial costs, these legal challenges can disrupt operations, diverting focus and resources away from the company's primary business objectives. Moreover, the public nature of lawsuits can lead to significant reputational harm, as the media and public often view these cases as indicative of deeper systemic issues within the organization.

In addition to the risk of lawsuits, companies that neglect DEI may also face penalties for failing to comply with antidiscrimination and equal opportunity laws. Regulatory bodies across various jurisdictions have established strict guidelines designed to ensure fair treatment in the workplace. Noncompliance can result in fines, sanctions, and other penalties that further strain the organization's financial and operational resources. For businesses operating across multiple regions, the complexity of adhering to different regulatory frameworks underscores the necessity of a strong DEI strategy.

1.6.2. Ethical Risks: Reputational Damage and the Erosion of Stakeholder Trust

While legal risks are often the most immediately apparent, the ethical risks of ignoring DEI can be even more detrimental in the long term. In today's socially conscious marketplace, a company's ethical stance on issues like diversity and inclusion plays a significant role in shaping its public image. Organizations that fail to demonstrate a commitment to DEI—or worse, that engage in or tolerate discriminatory practices—are likely to suffer severe reputational damage.

Reputational damage can manifest in several ways. Negative media coverage can spread quickly, particularly in the age of social media, where public opinion can shift rapidly. Companies may face boycotts, both online and in the marketplace, as consumers choose to support businesses that align with their values. The loss of customer loyalty can be particularly damaging, as it not only reduces immediate revenue but also undermines the longterm viability of the brand.

For publicly traded companies, the impact on reputation can extend to investor confidence. Ethical lapses, particularly those related to DEI, can lead to a decline in stock prices as investors reassess the company's leadership and ethical standards. Additionally, companies with damaged reputations may find it difficult to attract and retain top talent. Employees increasingly seek out employers who reflect their own values, and a perceived lack of commitment to DEI can lead to disengagement, higher turnover rates, and reduced productivity.

Stakeholder trust, once lost, is challenging to rebuild. Employees who perceive their workplace as unfair or exclusive may disengage, resulting in a toxic work environment that stifles innovation and collaboration. Customers, too, are likely to turn to competitors who are seen as more ethically aligned. Even investors may withdraw their support, leading to a loss of capital and market share.

1.6.3. Proactive DEI Strategies as Risk Mitigation

Given the significant legal and ethical risks associated with neglecting DEI, it is clear that a proactive approach is essential. Organizations that prioritize DEI not only mitigate these risks but also position themselves for longterm success. A strong DEI strategy involves more than just compliance with legal standards; it requires a commitment to fostering an inclusive culture that values diversity at every level.

Key components of a proactive DEI strategy include comprehensive training programs, transparent policies, and accountability mechanisms. Training programs should educate employees about the importance of DEI and provide them with the tools to recognize and address biases in the workplace. Transparent policies that outline the company's commitment to DEI, along with clear reporting and enforcement procedures, help build a culture of accountability. Additionally, regular assessments of DEI initiatives and outcomes ensure that the company remains on track and can make necessary adjustments as needed.

In conclusion, the risks associated with failing to address DEI are substantial and multifaceted. From the immediate threat of discrimination lawsuits to the longterm consequences of reputational damage, businesses that neglect DEI place themselves in a precarious position. However, by adopting a proactive approach to DEI, organizations can not only mitigate these risks but also unlock new opportunities for growth, innovation, and success.

As future business leaders, it is imperative for BBA and MBA students to understand the critical role that DEI plays in risk management. By integrating DEI into the core of business strategy, companies can protect themselves from legal and ethical pitfalls while building a foundation for sustainable success in an increasingly diverse and interconnected world.

1.7. Student Takeaway

DEI as a Strategic Advantage: Diversity, Equity, and Inclusion (DEI) is not merely a moral obligation; it is a powerful strategic advantage that can drive business success. By embedding DEI into the fabric of their business strategy, organizations can effectively mitigate legal and ethical risks, enhance their reputation, and build a more engaged and innovative workforce. For future business leaders, understanding and leveraging DEI is crucial for creating sustainable, competitive, and ethically responsible organizations in an increasingly globalized market.

Part 2: Understanding and Addressing Unconscious Bias

2.1. Unconscious Bias

Unconscious bias refers to the automatic, unintentional judgments or stereotypes we hold about people based on their race, gender, age, or other characteristics. These biases are formed over time through our experiences, culture, and media, and they can influence our behavior without us even realizing it.

In the workplace, unconscious bias can affect hiring decisions, promotions, team dynamics, and overall company culture. It's important to understand and address these biases to create a more inclusive and fair environment for everyone.

2.2. Common Types of Unconscious Bias

There are several types of unconscious bias that can show up in the workplace. Some of the most common include:

Affinity Bias: Favoring people who are similar to us in terms of background, interests, or experiences. For example, you might feel more comfortable working with someone who went to the same school as you.

Confirmation Bias: Seeking out or interpreting information in a way that confirms our preexisting beliefs. This can lead us to ignore evidence that contradicts our assumptions about others.

Gender Bias: Making assumptions about someone's abilities or interests based on their gender. For instance, assuming that a man is better suited for a leadership role than a woman.

Age Bias: Stereotyping someone based on their age, such as believing that older employees are less adaptable to change or that younger employees lack experience.

Halo Effect: Allowing one positive characteristic of a person to influence your overall perception of them. For example, if someone is very confident, you might assume they are also competent, even without evidence.

2.3. Impact of Unconscious Bias in the Workplace

Unconscious bias can have several negative effects on the workplace, including:

Inequitable Opportunities: Certain groups may be overlooked for promotions, training, or leadership roles due to biases, leading to an unfair distribution of opportunities.

Decreased Diversity: When biases influence hiring and promotion decisions, it can result in a less diverse workforce, which can limit creativity and innovation.

Lower Employee Morale: Employees who feel they are being treated unfairly due to biases may become disengaged, leading to lower job satisfaction and productivity.

Poor DecisionMaking: Decisions influenced by bias are often not based on objective criteria, leading to less effective outcomes for the organization.

2.4. Strategies for Identifying and Overcoming Unconscious Bias

Addressing unconscious bias requires awareness, education, and intentional action. Here are some strategies to help identify and overcome biases in the workplace:

Self Reflection: Encourage employees to reflect on their own biases and how these might influence their decisions. Regularly asking yourself questions like, "Am I being fair?" or "Would I make the same decision if this person were different in some way?" can help bring biases to light.

Bias Training: Provide training sessions that educate employees about unconscious bias, how it operates, and its impact on the workplace. These sessions should also offer practical tips for recognizing and mitigating bias.

Diverse Hiring Panels: Ensure that hiring and promotion decisions are made by diverse groups of people. This reduces the likelihood that one person's biases will dominate the decision making process.

Standardized Criteria: Use clear, objective criteria for hiring, promotions, and performance evaluations. This helps ensure that decisions are based on merit rather than subjective impressions.

Accountability Measures: Implement systems to track and review decisions related to hiring, promotions, and employee evaluations. This can help identify patterns of bias and hold decision makers accountable.

2.5. Building an Inclusive Workplace Culture

Overcoming unconscious bias is not just about individual actions; it's also about creating a workplace culture that values diversity and inclusion. Here are some ways to build such a culture:

Leadership Commitment: Leaders should model inclusive behavior and make diversity and inclusion a priority in the organization's values and goals.

Open Dialogue: Foster an environment where employees feel comfortable discussing bias and diversity issues. Open dialogue can help raise awareness and promote understanding.

Mentorship Programs: Establish mentorship programs that support employees from underrepresented groups. This can help ensure they have the guidance and opportunities needed to succeed.

Celebrate Diversity: Recognize and celebrate the diverse backgrounds and perspectives of your employees through events, initiatives, and communication.

Unconscious bias is a natural part of human behavior, but it can have significant negative effects in the workplace if left unchecked. By identifying and addressing these biases, organizations can create a more equitable, inclusive, and productive environment. This not only benefits employees but also contributes to the overall success of the organization. Understanding unconscious bias and taking steps to overcome it is essential for anyone aiming to build a fair and dynamic workplace.

2.6. Student Takeaway:

Unconscious bias affects workplace decisions and can lead to unfair opportunities and reduced diversity. By understanding common biases like affinity and gender bias, and using strategies like self reflection and bias training, we can create a more inclusive and equitable work environment.

Part 3: Introduction to Inclusive Culture

3.1. Inclusive Culture

An inclusive culture in the workplace means creating an environment where everyone feels they belong, are respected, and can contribute fully. It's about making sure that every employee, regardless of their background, feels valued and supported. An inclusive culture not only improves employee satisfaction but also boosts creativity, collaboration, and overall company success.

3.2. The Importance of Belonging and Respect

Belonging means that employees feel like they are an important part of the team, while respect means treating others with consideration and valuing their contributions. When employees feel they belong and are respected, they are more likely to be engaged, motivated, and loyal to the organization. This leads to better teamwork, higher productivity, and a positive work environment.

3.3. Strategies for Fostering a Culture of Belonging and Respect

Creating an inclusive culture requires intentional effort and specific strategies. Here are some effective ways to foster a culture of belonging and respect:

1. Lead by Example: Leaders and managers should model inclusive behavior by showing respect for all employees and valuing diverse perspectives. When leaders demonstrate inclusivity, it sets the tone for the entire organization.

2. Encourage Open Communication: Create an environment where employees feel safe to express their ideas, concerns, and feedback. Regularly seek input from all team members and listen to their perspectives. Open communication builds trust and ensures everyone's voice is heard.

3. Offer Diversity Training: Provide training programs that educate employees about the importance of diversity and inclusion. Training should cover topics like unconscious bias, cultural sensitivity, and how to create an inclusive environment.

4. Celebrate Differences: Recognize and celebrate the diverse backgrounds and experiences of your employees. This could include cultural events, awareness days, or simply acknowledging and appreciating the uniqueness of each team member.

5. Create Supportive Policies: Develop and implement policies that promote inclusion, such as flexible work arrangements, anti discrimination policies, and support for employee resource groups. These policies help ensure that everyone has equal access to opportunities and resources.

6. Promote Collaboration: Encourage teamwork and collaboration across different groups within the organization. When people from diverse backgrounds work together, they bring different ideas and perspectives, leading to more innovative solutions.

7. Provide Mentorship Opportunities: Establish mentorship programs where experienced employees can support and guide those from underrepresented groups. Mentorship helps build confidence, skills, and a sense of belonging for all participants.

3.4. Overcoming Challenges to Inclusion

Creating an inclusive culture is not without challenges. Resistance to change, unconscious biases, and a lack of understanding about the benefits of diversity can hinder progress. To overcome these challenges:

1. Educate Continuously: Ongoing education and training are crucial for changing mindsets and behaviors. Regularly update training programs and provide resources that help employees understand the value of inclusion.

2. Address Biases: Actively work to identify and reduce biases in the workplace. This can be done through regular assessments, feedback mechanisms, and creating accountability for inclusive behavior.

3. Support Change Agents: Identify and empower individuals within the organization who are passionate about inclusion. These change agents can help drive initiatives, educate others, and maintain momentum towards creating an inclusive culture.

3.5. Measuring Success in Building an Inclusive Culture

To know if your efforts to create an inclusive culture are working, it's important to measure success. Here are some ways to do that:

1. Employee Surveys: Conduct regular surveys to gather feedback from employees about how included and respected they feel. Use the results to identify areas for improvement.

2. Diversity Metrics: Track diversity at all levels of the organization, including recruitment, promotions, and retention rates. This helps ensure that the organization is making progress toward greater inclusivity.

3. Employee Engagement: Monitor employee engagement levels, as higher engagement is often linked to a more inclusive culture. Engaged employees are more likely to be productive, stay with the company, and contribute to a positive work environment.

4. Success Stories: Collect and share success stories of individuals or teams that have benefited from the inclusive culture. These stories can inspire others and highlight the positive impact of inclusivity on the organization.

Creating an inclusive culture is essential for fostering a workplace where everyone feels they belong and are respected. By implementing strategies such as leadership by example, open communication, diversity training, and supportive policies, organizations can build a more inclusive and productive environment. While challenges exist, continuous education, addressing biases, and measuring success are key to overcoming them. In doing so, companies not only enhance employee satisfaction but also drive innovation and success.

3.6. Student Takeaway:

An inclusive culture is crucial for creating a workplace where everyone feels valued and respected. By promoting open communication, offering diversity training, and implementing supportive policies, organizations can foster belonging and collaboration. Overcoming challenges like resistance and bias requires ongoing education and commitment. Measuring success through employee feedback and diversity metrics helps ensure continuous improvement and sustained inclusivity.

Part 4: Diversity Recruitment and Hiring Practices

4.1. Introduction to Diversity Recruitment

Diversity recruitment is the process of attracting and hiring employees from a wide range of backgrounds, including different races, genders, ages, abilities, and experiences. A diverse workforce brings varied perspectives, which can lead to more creativity, better problemsolving, and a stronger connection to a diverse customer base. However, to achieve true diversity, companies must be intentional in their recruitment and hiring practices.

4.2. The Importance of Diversity in Hiring

Hiring a diverse workforce is not only about fairness; it's also about building a stronger, more innovative company. When people from different backgrounds work together, they bring unique ideas and approaches to the table, which can lead to more effective solutions and a competitive edge in the market. Moreover, diverse teams are often more adaptable and better at meeting the needs of a diverse customer base. Companies that prioritize diversity in hiring also enhance their reputation, making them more attractive to top talent.

4.3. Best Practices for Attracting Diverse Talent

To attract a diverse pool of candidates, companies need to be proactive and strategic in their recruitment efforts. Here are some best practices:

1. Broaden Your Outreach: Advertise job openings in a variety of places, including job boards that target underrepresented groups, professional associations, and community organizations. This helps reach a wider and more diverse audience.

2. Use Inclusive Language: Ensure that job descriptions and advertisements use inclusive language that appeals to a broad audience. Avoid jargon or phrases that might unintentionally exclude certain groups. For example, terms like "rockstar" or "ninja" might deter some candidates.

3. Showcase Diversity: Highlight your company's commitment to diversity and inclusion in your job postings, website, and social media. Showcase diverse teams and share stories of how your company values and supports diversity. This can make your company more appealing to candidates from different backgrounds.

4. Partner with Diverse Organizations: Build relationships with schools, universities, and professional organizations that serve underrepresented groups. Participate in job fairs, mentoring programs, and other events that connect you with diverse talent.

5. Create Internship and Apprenticeship Programs: Offer internships or apprenticeships that are specifically designed to attract candidates from diverse backgrounds. These programs can provide valuable experience and serve as a pipeline for future hires.

4.4. Best Practices for Selecting Diverse Talent

Once you have attracted a diverse pool of candidates, it's important to ensure that your selection process is fair and unbiased. Here are some best practices:

1. Standardize the Interview Process: Use a standardized interview process with consistent questions for all candidates. This reduces the risk of bias and ensures that all candidates are evaluated on the same criteria.

2. Use Diverse Interview Panels: Include a diverse group of people on interview panels. This can help reduce bias in the selection process and provide a more balanced evaluation of candidates.

3. Focus on Skills and Potential: When evaluating candidates, focus on their skills, experience, and potential rather than relying on "culture fit." Consider how a candidate's unique background and experiences could contribute to the team.

4. Blind Hiring Techniques: Consider using blind hiring techniques, such as removing names, gender, and other identifying information from resumes during the initial screening process. This can help reduce unconscious bias and ensure that candidates are evaluated based on their qualifications.

5. Evaluate and Improve: Continuously evaluate your recruitment and selection processes to identify and address any biases. Collect feedback from candidates and hiring managers to make improvements and ensure that your practices are as inclusive as possible.

4.5. Overcoming Challenges in Diversity Recruitment

Recruiting diverse talent can come with challenges, such as overcoming biases, finding diverse candidates, and ensuring retention after hiring. Here's how to address these challenges:

1. Address Biases: Provide training for hiring managers and interviewers on recognizing and reducing unconscious bias. This helps create a more fair and inclusive selection process.

2. Expand Talent Pools: If you're struggling to find diverse candidates, consider expanding your talent pool by looking beyond traditional sources. Explore different regions, industries, and backgrounds that you may not have considered before.

3. Retention Strategies: Once diverse talent is hired, focus on retention by creating an inclusive work environment where everyone feels valued and supported. Offer mentorship programs, career development opportunities, and ensure that your company culture is welcoming to all.

Diversity recruitment and hiring are essential for building a strong, innovative, and competitive workforce. By adopting best practices such as broadening outreach, standardizing the interview process, and using inclusive language, companies can attract and select diverse talent. Overcoming challenges like bias and retention requires ongoing commitment and effort, but the benefits—ranging from enhanced creativity to a better connection with customers—make it well worth the investment.

4.6. Student Takeaway:

Diversity in recruitment and hiring strengthens a company by bringing in varied perspectives and fostering innovation. To attract diverse talent, use inclusive language, broaden outreach, and showcase your commitment to diversity. In the selection process, standardize interviews, focus on skills, and reduce bias. Overcoming challenges like unconscious bias and retention requires ongoing effort, but the benefits of a diverse and inclusive workforce are significant and longlasting.

Part 5: Equitable Talent Management and Development

5.1. Introduction

In any organization, ensuring that all employees have the same chances to learn, grow, and advance is critical for both fairness and success. Equitable talent management focuses on providing fair opportunities for all employees, especially those from underrepresented groups. By creating an inclusive environment where everyone can thrive, companies can tap into the full potential of their workforce.

5.2. Equitable Development

What is Equitable Development?

Equitable development means giving all employees equal access to careerbuilding opportunities such as training programs, mentoring, and leadership development. Not everyone starts with the same advantages or networks, so companies need to make sure that opportunities are available to everyone, especially those who may face barriers in their careers.

Why is it important?

Without equitable development, some employees may not get the same opportunities to advance. This can lead to a lack of diversity in higher positions, which not only affects individuals but also limits the company's ability to benefit from diverse perspectives.

How can organizations promote equitable development?

- **Training and Development Programs:** Organizations should offer accessible and wellstructured training programs for all employees. This helps ensure that everyone, regardless of their background, has the opportunity to develop their skills and advance.

- **Mentorship Programs:** Mentorship is a powerful way to provide support and guidance to employees. Companies should actively connect mentors with employees from underrepresented groups to ensure they have the support needed to grow their careers.

- **Leadership Development:** Create programs that help diverse employees prepare for leadership roles by teaching them essential management skills and providing networking opportunities.

5.3. Performance Management

What is Performance Management?

Performance management is the process of evaluating employees' work and giving them feedback to help them improve. This process needs to be fair and free from bias so that all employees have equal chances to succeed.

Why is bias in performance evaluations a problem?

If performance evaluations are biased, certain employees may not be recognized for their contributions, which can prevent them from advancing. Bias can be based on factors like gender, race, or cultural background and often happens unconsciously.

How can companies ensure fair evaluations?

- **Standardized Evaluation Criteria:** Use clear, objective criteria for evaluating performance, rather than relying on subjective opinions. This helps reduce bias and ensures that all employees are evaluated on the same basis.
- **Training for Managers:** Managers should be trained to recognize and reduce their unconscious biases when giving feedback and conducting performance reviews.
- **Regular Feedback:** Providing ongoing feedback throughout the year, rather than just during annual reviews, helps employees improve and stay on track. This also prevents biases from creeping into lastminute assessments.

5.4. Succession Planning

What is Succession Planning?

Succession planning is about identifying and preparing employees to move into leadership positions. It's important for ensuring that companies have diverse leadership teams and that everyone has an equal chance to advance.

Why is it important for equity?

Often, the same groups of people are selected for leadership roles, which means that talented individuals from diverse backgrounds may be overlooked. A more equitable approach to succession planning ensures that underrepresented groups are considered for leadership positions.

How can companies create an equitable succession plan?

- **Identify HighPotential Employees:** Look for highpotential employees across all departments and from different backgrounds, not just those who fit the traditional mold of a leader.
- **Offer Leadership Development Programs:** Provide training programs that help diverse employees develop the skills needed to move into leadership roles.

- **Create Diverse Leadership Pipelines:** Ensure that the pool of candidates being prepared for leadership positions reflects the diversity of the workforce. This will lead to more inclusive leadership teams in the future.

Equitable talent management and development is crucial for creating a fair and inclusive workplace. By providing equal access to development opportunities, ensuring fair performance evaluations, and including diverse candidates in succession planning, companies can ensure that all employees have the chance to succeed. When employees feel valued and see real opportunities for growth, they are more engaged and motivated, which ultimately benefits the entire organization.

5.5. Student Takeaway:

Equity in talent management ensures that all employees, regardless of background, have the opportunity to grow, succeed, and contribute to the organization.

Part 6: Addressing Microaggressions and Workplace Conflict

6.1. Understanding Microaggressions

Microaggressions are subtle, often unintentional, actions or comments that convey negative, stereotypical, or discriminatory messages toward individuals from marginalized groups. Unlike overt discrimination, microaggressions are typically less obvious and can be easily dismissed as harmless, but their impact is cumulative and damaging.

6.2. Types of Microaggressions:

- Verbal Microaggressions: These are subtle, sometimes well meaning comments that can be offensive or dismissive. For example, asking an employee of Asian descent, "Where are you really from?" implies that they are not truly part of the community.
- NonVerbal Microaggressions: This includes actions or behaviors, such as repeatedly interrupting a woman during a meeting or making assumptions about someone's abilities based on their appearance.

Environmental Microaggressions: These occur when workplaces or institutions unintentionally promote stereotypes or reinforce exclusion. An example might be an office where all the leadership positions are held by individuals from the same race or gender.

6.3. Impact of Microaggressions:

- ✓ Emotional and Psychological Toll: Microaggressions can lead to feelings of alienation, anxiety, and decreased morale. Even if each microaggression seems small, repeated incidents can create an oppressive environment for those experiencing them.

- ✓ Damage to Inclusion: Microaggressions signal to employees that they are "outsiders" or not fully accepted. Over time, this undermines their sense of belonging, resulting in disengagement, lower productivity, and higher turnover rates.

Recognizing microaggressions is the first step toward addressing them. Awareness among both leadership and staff is essential to ensuring a truly inclusive culture.

6.4. Conflict Resolution

Conflicts related to DEI often arise from miscommunication or differences in cultural expectations. These conflicts can escalate when microaggressions go unaddressed or when there is a lack of understanding about diversity related issues. Resolving these conflicts effectively is critical for maintaining harmony in the workplace.

Identifying the Source of Conflict:

DEI related conflicts may stem from misunderstandings or biased assumptions. For example, a conflict could arise when an employee feels slighted by comments that reflect unconscious bias or stereotypes.

It's essential to identify whether the conflict is rooted in cultural differences, communication styles, or implicit bias. Understanding the source of tension is key to addressing it.

Strategies for Conflict Resolution:

- ✓ Open Dialogue: Encourage employees to engage in honest, nonconfrontational conversations about their concerns. Giving employees the space to share their experiences and perspectives can help diffuse tension before it escalates.

- ✓ Mediation: In cases where conflict persists, involving a neutral mediator—such as an HR professional trained in DEI issues—can help both parties better understand each other and find a resolution. Mediators guide the conversation toward common ground, facilitating a deeper understanding of the underlying issues.

- ✓ Setting Clear Expectations: Establish guidelines for respectful behavior and communication in the workplace. Setting the standard for how employees should address conflicts can create a healthier and more respectful working environment.

Effective conflict resolution doesn't just solve immediate issues but also builds the foundation for a more inclusive and respectful workplace. Addressing conflicts as they arise helps employees feel heard and supported.

6.5. Promoting Respectful Communication

Fostering an environment where open and respectful communication is encouraged is a key part of preventing and addressing microaggressions and DEI related conflicts.

Cultural Sensitivity Training: Educating employees about cultural differences and the impact of microaggressions can create greater awareness and reduce the likelihood of unintentionally harmful behaviors. These training sessions can help employees recognize their unconscious biases and develop more inclusive communication habits.

Active Listening: Encourage employees to practice active listening, where they fully focus on understanding others' perspectives without judgment or interruption. When team members listen to each other with empathy, it leads to stronger relationships and a more inclusive environment.

Encouraging Feedback: Create an environment where employees feel comfortable giving and receiving feedback about DEI issues. For instance, if someone notices a microaggression, they should feel safe bringing it up without fear of retaliation or dismissal. Feedback should be encouraged in a constructive, non confrontational way.

Building a workplace culture where respectful communication is the norm helps prevent the misunderstandings and biases that can lead to conflict. It also empowers employees to speak up and address issues before they become bigger problems.

6.6. Student Takeaway:

Addressing microaggressions and DEI related conflicts proactively is essential for creating a respectful and inclusive workplace. By fostering open, respectful communication and implementing effective conflict resolution strategies, organizations can create an environment where all employees feel valued, respected, and heard.

Part 7: Leveraging Employee Resource Groups (ERGs) for DEI

7.1. Role of ERGs:

- Employee Resource Groups are voluntary, employee led groups that focus on specific shared characteristics or life experiences such as race, gender, sexual orientation, disability, or veteran status. They play a critical role in helping organizations advance their DEI goals by providing support, advocacy, and insights on the needs of underrepresented groups.

- Supporting Underrepresented Employees: ERGs create a sense of community for individuals who may feel marginalized in the broader workplace. For example, an ERG for women in leadership can provide mentorship, guidance, and support to help women advance in their careers.

- Advocating for Change: ERGs act as internal advocates, providing feedback to leadership on DEI policies and practices. They can influence company decisions related to inclusion, equity, and diversity by offering a direct perspective on the unique challenges faced by certain groups.

- Driving Awareness and Education: ERGs help raise awareness about the importance of DEI by organizing events, workshops, and discussions. This helps foster a culture of inclusion across the organization.

7.2. Benefits of ERGs:

ERGs offer several benefits to both employees and the organization as a whole.

- Enhancing Employee Engagement: ERGs provide employees with an opportunity to contribute beyond their day-to-day work, increasing their sense of belonging and engagement. Employees who feel represented and heard are more likely to be motivated, productive, and loyal to the organization.

- Fostering Networking and Career Development: ERGs often organize events like mentorship programs, career workshops, and networking sessions, which help members develop professionally. For instance, a multicultural ERG might provide networking opportunities that connect members to senior leaders across the company.

- Driving Cultural Change: ERGs help influence the organization's culture by promoting diversity and inclusion. By elevating the voices of underrepresented groups, ERGs encourage the company to make decisions that foster a more inclusive environment for all employees.

7.3. Supporting ERGs:

For ERGs to thrive and effectively contribute to DEI efforts, organizations must provide adequate support.

- Providing Resources and Funding: Organizations should allocate resources, including financial support and dedicated time, for ERG activities. This ensures that ERGs can organize events, provide training, and carry out initiatives that align with DEI objectives.

- Leadership Involvement: ERGs need support from senior leadership to have a meaningful impact. When executives actively participate in ERG activities, it signals to the entire organization that DEI is a priority. Leaders can act as sponsors for ERGs, providing mentorship and ensuring that ERG voices are heard in decision making processes.

- Recognizing Contributions: Recognizing the contributions of ERGs and their members is key to sustaining momentum. Publicly acknowledging the work of ERGs, whether through awards, promotions, or public recognition, reinforces the importance of DEI efforts and encourages greater participation.

7.4. Student Takeaway:

Employee Resource Groups are powerful tools for driving DEI initiatives and creating a more inclusive workplace. They support underrepresented employees, foster engagement and networking, and help influence cultural change within the organization. For ERGs to be successful, organizations must provide the necessary support through resources, leadership involvement, and recognition of their contributions.

Part 8: Measuring and Tracking DEI Progress

8.1. Importance of Metrics:

Measuring DEI initiatives is essential for understanding their impact and identifying areas for improvement. Without data, it's challenging to know if DEI efforts are making a difference.

Accountability: Tracking DEI progress ensures that leaders are held accountable for advancing DEI goals. When metrics are tied to performance, DEI becomes a priority across the organization.

Informed Decision Making: Data helps identify gaps or disparities within the organization. For instance, if women are underrepresented in leadership positions, the data will highlight this issue and allow the organization to implement targeted strategies to address it.

Continuous Improvement: Measuring DEI initiatives allows organizations to assess what's working and what's not, leading to better outcomes over time. Regular reviews of DEI metrics ensure that the organization continues to evolve and adapt its strategies.

8.2. Key Metrics:

To measure DEI effectively, organizations should track a variety of metrics related to diversity, equity, and inclusion.

Diversity Ratios: These metrics measure the representation of different demographic groups (e.g., gender, race, age) across all levels of the organization, from entry level to leadership. Diversity ratios help identify any under representation within the company.

Employee Engagement Scores: Engagement surveys provide insights into how employees feel about the organization's commitment to DEI. High engagement scores among diverse groups indicate a positive, inclusive culture, while lower scores suggest that more work needs to be done.

Retention Rates: Monitoring the retention rates of diverse employees is crucial to understanding whether the organization is successful in creating an environment where all employees feel valued and included. High turnover rates among certain groups may signal issues with inclusion or equity.

8.3. Using Data:

Once data has been collected, organizations need to use it to drive action and improvement.

Identifying Areas for Improvement: Data reveals where the organization may be falling short in its DEI efforts. For example, if women are underrepresented in certain departments, the company can take steps to address hiring and promotion practices in those areas.

Setting DEI Goals: Based on the metrics, organizations can set specific, measurable goals for improvement. For instance, they may aim to increase the representation of underrepresented groups in leadership roles by a certain percentage within a set time frame.

Communicating Progress: Sharing DEI metrics with employees, stakeholders, and the public demonstrates transparency and reinforces the organization's commitment to DEI. It also helps build trust within the company and encourages accountability at all levels.

8.4. Student Takeaway:

Measuring and tracking DEI progress is essential for ensuring that DEI initiatives are effective and aligned with organizational goals. Using metrics like diversity ratios, employee engagement scores, and retention rates, organizations can identify areas for improvement and ensure accountability in their DEI efforts.

Part 9: Leading with Empathy and Courage

9.1. Empathetic Leadership:

Empathy is the ability to understand and share the feelings of others. In the context of DEI, empathetic leadership means recognizing the unique experiences and challenges faced by diverse employees.

- ➤ Understanding Employee Experiences: Leaders should take the time to listen to employees from underrepresented groups and understand their perspectives. Empathy helps leaders identify barriers to inclusion and find solutions to overcome them.

- ➤ Building Trust and Connection: Empathetic leaders foster trust by showing employees that they genuinely care about their well being. This trust creates a safe space where employees feel comfortable sharing their experiences and concerns.

9.2. Courageous Leadership:

Driving meaningful change in DEI requires leaders to be courageous in addressing challenges and pushing the organization forward.

- ➤ Tackling Difficult Conversations: Leaders must be willing to engage in uncomfortable conversations about race, gender, and other DEI related issues. This requires courage, as these discussions can be sensitive and challenging to navigate.

- ➤ Taking Bold Actions: Courageous leaders are not afraid to make decisions that may be unpopular but are necessary for creating a more equitable and inclusive workplace. For example, implementing policies that prioritize diversity in hiring or promotions may face resistance, but they are essential for driving change.

Leading by Example:

Leaders must model inclusive behaviors to set the tone for the rest of the organization. When employees see their leaders actively championing DEI, they are more likely to follow suit.

9.3. Inclusive Leadership:

This involves being mindful of how decisions impact diverse employees, promoting collaboration, and valuing different perspectives. Leaders should demonstrate respect, fairness, and inclusion in their daily interactions. Advocating for DEI: Leaders can advocate for DEI by supporting DEI initiatives, participating in training, and ensuring that DEI remains a priority in organizational decision making.

9.4. Student Takeaway:

Effective DEI leadership requires empathy, courage, and a commitment to driving positive change. By understanding the experiences of diverse employees, engaging in difficult conversations, and modeling inclusive behavior, leaders can create a more inclusive and equitable workplace.

Part 10: Sustaining DEI Momentum and Overcoming Resistance

10.1. Maintaining Momentum:

Sustaining DEI progress requires continuous effort, even after initial success. It's important to keep DEI initiatives active and evolving.

Continuous Learning: Organizations must stay informed about new DEI trends, research, and best practices. Regular training and education ensure that employees and leaders remain aware of DEI challenges and solutions.

Adapting Strategies: DEI efforts should be flexible and adaptable to the changing needs of the workforce and external environment. For example, organizations may need to adjust their DEI goals based on shifts in the demographic makeup of the company.

10.2. Embedding DEI into Organizational

Culture: To sustain momentum, DEI must be deeply embedded in the company's culture, values, and policies. This includes ensuring that DEI principles are reflected in all aspects of the business, from hiring to performance evaluations.

10.3. Overcoming Resistance:

Resistance to DEI initiatives can come from various sources, including employees who are uncomfortable with change or leaders who are skeptical of the benefits of DEI.

Addressing Employee Concerns: Resistance often stems from fear or misunderstanding. Providing clear communication about the purpose and benefits of DEI can help alleviate concerns and build support for DEI initiatives.

Engaging Leadership: Leaders who resist DEI efforts may need more education on the business case for DEI. Providing them with data and case studies that demonstrate the positive impact of DEI can help shift their perspective.

Creating Accountability: Holding leaders and employees accountable for DEI progress is crucial for overcoming resistance. Tying DEI goals to performance evaluations and rewards can incentivize commitment to DEI initiatives.

10.4. Student Takeaway:

Sustaining DEI momentum requires continuous learning, adapting strategies, and embedding DEI into organizational culture. Overcoming resistance is essential for long term success, and organizations must address concerns and hold leaders accountable to ensure progress.

Glossary of Key Terms in Managing Diversity, Equity and Inclusion

I. Diversity: The presence of differences within a given setting, including race, ethnicity, gender, age, sexual orientation, disability, socioeconomic background, and other characteristics that contribute to the uniqueness of individuals.

II. Equity: The fair treatment, access, opportunity, and advancement for all individuals, while striving to identify and eliminate barriers that have historically led to unequal treatment.

III. Inclusion: The practice of creating environments in which any individual or group can be and feel welcomed, respected, supported, and valued. It involves actively involving diverse groups in decision-making processes and ensuring everyone has a voice.

IV. Implicit Bias: Unconscious attitudes or stereotypes that affect our understanding, actions, and decisions. These biases can influence judgments about people based on race, gender, or other characteristics without our awareness.

V. Cultural Competence: The ability to interact effectively with people of different cultures, understanding and respecting cultural differences, and adapting one's approach accordingly.

VI. Microaggressions: Everyday, subtle, unintentional, and oftentimes dismissive interactions or behaviors that perpetuate stereotypes or demean individuals based on their identity or background.

VII. Intersectionality: A framework for understanding how various aspects of a person's identity (e.g., race, gender, class, sexuality) intersect and influence their experiences of oppression or privilege.

VIII. Affirmative Action: Policies and practices designed to promote the representation and inclusion of marginalized groups in areas such as employment and education, aiming to counteract historical inequalities.

IX. Accessibility: The design of products, environments, and services to be usable by people with disabilities, ensuring equal access and participation.

X. Diversity Training: Educational programs aimed at increasing awareness of diversity issues, reducing biases, and developing skills to foster a more inclusive workplace or community.

Chapter 3: Managing Employee Engagement

Part: 1. Introduction

Employee engagement refers to an employee's emotional commitment and connection toward their organization and its goals. It involves more than just job satisfaction; engaged employees are deeply invested in their work, often going above and beyond their job requirements. This dedication contributes to the organization's overall success, fostering a culture of productivity, innovation, and collaboration.

1.1 Definition of Employee Engagement

Employee engagement is defined as the level of enthusiasm and dedication an employee feels toward their work and the organization they belong to. It involves employees who are fully absorbed by and enthusiastic about their work and take positive action to further the organization's interests. Engaged employees demonstrate high commitment, are aligned with the company's vision, and are driven to help the organization achieve its goals.

Unlike job satisfaction, which only measures how content employees are with their work, engagement measures their emotional involvement and willingness to go the extra mile for the organization. An engaged employee is motivated to perform well and actively seeks opportunities to contribute to the company's long-term success.

1.2 Importance of Employee Engagement in Organizational Success

Employee engagement plays a critical role in determining the success of an organization. Numerous studies show that higher levels of engagement are associated with increased productivity, profitability, and customer satisfaction, while lower engagement levels can lead to high turnover, absenteeism, and reduced performance. Engaged employees are more likely to be loyal, stay with the company longer, and actively advocate for the organization, thus enhancing its internal and external reputation.

The impact of employee engagement extends beyond individual performance. Engaged employees create a positive work culture that encourages collaboration, creativity, and resilience. They are more likely to support their colleagues and contribute to an environment that drives innovation and continuous improvement. In contrast, disengaged employees can negatively affect team dynamics and productivity, leading to higher costs and lost opportunities for growth.

Furthermore, employee engagement contributes to customer satisfaction. Employees who are engaged are more likely to provide better service, which results in stronger customer relationships and loyalty. Thus, managing engagement effectively is essential for maintaining competitive advantage and driving sustainable success.

Overview of Employee Engagement Management

Managing employee engagement involves the deliberate actions taken by leadership and management to foster a work environment where employees feel valued, supported, and motivated. It includes setting clear goals, recognizing employee contributions, providing opportunities for growth, and ensuring open communication across all levels of the organization. Managers play a key role in this process by understanding individual employee needs and aligning them with organizational goals.

The process of managing engagement begins with measuring employee attitudes and perceptions through surveys and feedback mechanisms. Based on these insights, organizations can implement strategies to enhance engagement, such as leadership development, team-building initiatives, career development programs, and performance recognition systems.

In the modern workplace, engagement management must also take into account challenges such as remote work, cultural diversity, and generational differences. Organizations that adapt to these factors and maintain a focus on the well-being and growth of their employees are better equipped to cultivate high levels of engagement. By investing in employee engagement, organizations can ensure that they retain top talent, improve business outcomes, and maintain a thriving, productive workforce.

Part 2: Theories of Employee Engagement

Several theories provide insight into how employee engagement can be cultivated within an organization. One of the widely recognized models is the **Engagement Pyramid**, which represents a hierarchy of needs and factors that influence an employee's level of engagement. This pyramid builds on the concept that engagement is driven by both individual and organizational factors, progressing from meeting basic needs to aligning personal goals with the organization's mission.

2.1. The Engagement Pyramid

The Engagement Pyramid is a hierarchical model designed to understand and address the various levels of employee needs that contribute to their overall engagement. Similar to Maslow's Hierarchy of Needs, this model posits that employees become progressively more engaged as their foundational needs are met and their relationship with the organization deepens. The pyramid is composed of four levels:

Basic Needs

At the base of the Engagement Pyramid are the **basic needs** that must be fulfilled for employees to feel secure and comfortable in their roles. These include the physical and psychological requirements for employees to perform their jobs effectively:

Clarity of Role and Expectations: Employees need to understand what is expected of them, including clear job descriptions, goals, and responsibilities. Without this clarity, employees may feel uncertain or anxious, which can hinder engagement.

Access to Resources: Employees must have the necessary tools, technology, and resources to carry out their tasks efficiently. Without adequate resources, employees may feel frustrated or unable to perform to the best of their abilities.

Fair Compensation: While financial rewards alone do not guarantee engagement, employees expect fair compensation for their work. Ensuring that employees feel fairly compensated is essential for fostering a sense of security and commitment.

When these basic needs are not met, it becomes difficult for employees to engage at higher levels within the organization. Ensuring that these foundational requirements are addressed is the first step toward building a more engaged workforce.

Individual Contributions

Once basic needs are satisfied, employees seek to contribute as individuals within the organization. This level focuses on employees' personal sense of contribution, fulfillment, and growth:

Recognition of Efforts: Employees who feel their contributions are acknowledged and valued are likelier to be engaged. Regular formal or informal recognition helps reinforce a sense of accomplishment and motivation.

Opportunities for Growth: Employees who see opportunities for personal and professional development are more likely to stay engaged. Offering training, mentorship, and career advancement opportunities can help employees feel that their organization is invested in their long-term success.

Autonomy and Empowerment: Employees want to have control over how they approach their work. By granting autonomy and empowering employees to make decisions, organizations can foster a sense of ownership and accountability, which is key to enhancing engagement.

At this stage, employees are motivated by their ability to contribute meaningfully to the organization. They feel valued for their skills and efforts and are motivated to continue performing at high levels.

Team Support

The third level of the pyramid emphasizes the importance of **team support** and collaboration in building engagement. Humans are inherently social, and the quality of relationships in the workplace plays a significant role in determining engagement levels:

Collaboration and Teamwork: Employees are more engaged when they feel supported by their team members and work in a collaborative environment. Teams that communicate effectively, trust one another, and share responsibilities tend to foster higher levels of engagement.

Peer Recognition: In addition to recognition from managers, employees value recognition from their peers. Positive feedback and appreciation within teams strengthen relationships and contribute to a supportive work culture.

Psychological Safety: Employees need to feel safe to express their ideas, ask questions, and take risks without fear of punishment or judgment. A psychologically safe environment promotes innovation and encourages active participation in team efforts.

At this level, employees are not only focused on their own performance but also on contributing to their team's success. A positive team dynamic creates a sense of belonging and shared purpose, which is critical for sustained engagement.

Organizational Alignment

At the top of the Engagement Pyramid is organizational alignment, where employees' values, goals, and motivations align with those of the organization. This level is characterized by:

Shared Vision and Purpose: Employees who believe in the organization's mission and understand how their work contributes to its success are more engaged. Clear communication of the organization's vision and purpose helps employees feel that they are part of something bigger than themselves.

Cultural Fit: Employees who feel that they fit well within the organizational culture are more likely to be engaged. Organizations that foster inclusive, values-driven cultures tend to see higher engagement rates.

Leadership Trust and Transparency: Trust in leadership is essential for high engagement. Employees who trust their leaders, feel treated fairly, and perceive transparency in decision-making are more likely to be committed to the organization's success.

At this highest level, employees are not only contributing to their individual and team goals but are also aligned with the overall vision and mission of the organization. They feel a deep connection to the company's purpose and are motivated to contribute to its long-term success.

The Engagement Pyramid illustrates that employee engagement is not achieved overnight; it is a process that begins with addressing basic needs and gradually builds toward a deeper connection between the employee and the organization. Organizations can create a more engaged and motivated workforce by understanding and managing these levels.

2.2. Self-Determination Theory

Self-Determination Theory (SDT) is a psychological framework that explains human motivation and how different factors contribute to an individual's sense of engagement, well-being, and productivity. Developed by psychologists Edward Deci and Richard Ryan, SDT focuses on three fundamental psychological needs—**autonomy**, **competence**, and **relatedness**—that must be satisfied to promote intrinsic motivation and engagement. In the context of employee engagement, SDT helps explain how organizations can create an environment where employees feel motivated, empowered, and engaged in their work.

- Autonomy

refers to the need to feel in control of one's own actions and decisions. When employees have autonomy, they experience a sense of ownership and responsibility, enhancing motivation and engagement. Autonomy doesn't mean employees are left to work in isolation, but rather that they are trusted to decide how to accomplish their tasks.

Freedom of Choice: Employees who are given the freedom to choose how they approach their tasks are more likely to feel engaged. This could involve having control over how they organize their workday, choose their projects, or solve problems.

Empowerment: Empowering employees to make decisions and take ownership of their work fosters a deeper sense of involvement. Employees who feel trusted by their managers are more likely to take initiative and put forth their best effort.

Flexible Work Arrangements: Offering flexible work options, such as remote work or flexible hours, can enhance feelings of autonomy. Employees often feel more engaged and satisfied when they can structure their work around personal preferences or responsibilities.

Autonomy is a key driver of intrinsic motivation, which is the desire to perform a task because it is inherently rewarding rather than because of external pressures or rewards. Employees with higher levels of autonomy tend to be more creative, productive, and engaged in their roles.

- Competence

refers to the need to feel capable and effective in one's work. When employees believe they are skilled and have the ability to perform their tasks successfully, they are more likely to feel engaged. Competence involves both having the skills necessary to do the job and the opportunity to grow and develop those skills further.

Mastery and Skill Development: Employees are more engaged when they have opportunities to build their skills and master new areas of their work. Providing access to training, development programs, and challenging assignments helps employees feel that they are growing and becoming more competent in their roles.

Clear Feedback: Regular, constructive feedback is essential for fostering a sense of competence. When employees receive feedback that highlights their strengths and areas for improvement, they feel more confident in their abilities and are more likely to engage with their work.

Achievable Challenges: Setting challenging yet attainable goals gives employees the opportunity to demonstrate their competence. When employees overcome these challenges, they experience a sense of accomplishment and pride, which boosts engagement.

When employees feel competent, they are more motivated to continue improving and contributing to the organization. This sense of mastery and effectiveness enhances their engagement and long-term commitment to the organization.

- Relatedness

is the need to feel connected to others and to be part of a larger community. Employees who feel a sense of belonging and connection with their coworkers, managers, and the organization as a whole are more likely to be engaged. Relatedness fosters emotional bonds that motivate employees to invest in their work and the success of the organization.

Positive Relationships: Engaged employees often have strong, positive relationships with their colleagues and supervisors. When employees feel supported and valued by their team, they are more likely to be motivated and committed to their work.

Sense of Belonging: Employees who feel that they are part of a larger community and that their contributions matter to the organization tend to experience higher levels of engagement. This sense of belonging can be cultivated through team-building activities, open communication, and an inclusive organizational culture.

Supportive Work Environment: A supportive environment where employees can collaborate, seek help, and share their experiences fosters a sense of relatedness. When employees feel they are part of a team and that they can rely on others, it strengthens their emotional connection to the organization.

Relatedness helps to create a sense of loyalty and commitment, as employees are more likely to engage with an organization where they feel emotionally connected to others.

In summary, Self-Determination Theory suggests that employee engagement is driven by fulfilling the psychological needs for autonomy, competence, and relatedness. When organizations create an environment that supports these needs, employees are more likely to experience intrinsic motivation, leading to higher levels of engagement, performance, and satisfaction. By focusing on these three elements, managers can build a work culture that promotes sustainable engagement and fosters long-term organizational success.

2.3. Job Demands-Resources Model (JD-R Model)

The Job Demands-Resources Model (JD-R Model) is a framework that explains the factors influencing employee well-being, engagement, and performance in the workplace. Developed by Arnold Bakker and Evangelia Demerouti, the JD-R Model focuses on the balance between job demands and job resources, suggesting that while high demands can lead to stress and burnout, the availability of sufficient resources can enhance motivation and engagement.

This model is widely used to understand how work-related factors contribute to both negative outcomes, such as burnout, and positive outcomes, such as employee engagement.

Job Demands vs. Job Resources

In the JD-R Model, the workplace is viewed through two primary categories:

- Job Demands: These are the physical, psychological, social, or organizational aspects of the job that require sustained effort and energy. Job demands are not necessarily negative, but they can lead to stress and burnout when they are excessive or prolonged. Examples include:

- Workload: Heavy workloads or tight deadlines can create pressure and stress for employees.

- Emotional Demands: Roles that require emotional labor, such as managing customer relationships or dealing with stressful situations, can be mentally taxing.

- Role Conflict or Ambiguity: Unclear job roles, conflicting expectations, or a lack of role clarity can increase frustration and anxiety for employees.

- Time Pressure: Continuous pressure to meet deadlines or manage multiple tasks can result in fatigue and decreased well-being.

- Job Resources: These are the physical, psychological, social, or organizational aspects of the job that help employees cope with job demands and enhance their ability to achieve work goals. Job resources not only reduce the impact of job demands but also foster engagement and motivation. Examples include:

- Supportive Leadership: Leaders who provide clear guidance, encouragement, and feedback can help reduce stress and increase motivation.

- Autonomy: Having control over one's work and decision-making enhances a sense of ownership and engagement.

- Opportunities for Growth: Access to training, development, and career progression helps employees feel valued and motivated.

- Positive Work Environment: A work culture that promotes collaboration, trust, and respect among colleagues strengthens employee well-being.

The key principle of the JD-R Model is that while job demands can deplete an employee's energy, job resources act as protective factors that not only mitigate the negative effects of demands but also enhance motivation and engagement.

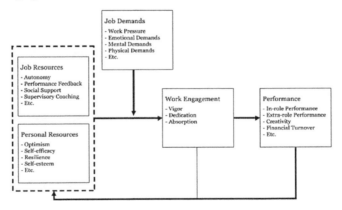

The JD-R model of work engagement (Source: (Bakker, Hakanen, Demerouti, & Xanthopoulou, 2007)

Impact on Employee Burnout and Engagement

The JD-R Model explains two main processes that influence employee well-being:

1. Health Impairment Process (Burnout):

- When job demands are high and not sufficiently counterbalanced by job resources, employees experience excessive strain. Over time, this strain leads to exhaustion, stress, and ultimately burnout. Burnout is characterized by emotional exhaustion, depersonalization, and a reduced sense of personal accomplishment.

- Employees who experience burnout are likely to exhibit negative behaviors such as disengagement, absenteeism, and reduced productivity. For example, an employee facing excessive workloads with little support or recognition may feel overwhelmed and disengage from their tasks.

- The health impairment process emphasizes the importance of managing job demands and ensuring that they do not exceed employees' coping capacity.

2. Motivational Process (Engagement):

- On the positive side, when job resources are plentiful, they can foster a sense of motivation and engagement. Resources such as supportive leadership, career development opportunities, and job autonomy empower employees to excel in their roles.

- Engaged employees are characterized by high energy levels, dedication to their work, and a sense of involvement and fulfillment. They are more likely to take initiative, solve problems creatively, and contribute positively to the organization's goals.

- The motivational process highlights that job resources are critical for building and sustaining engagement, even in the face of high job demands. For instance, an employee with a heavy workload may remain highly engaged if they have autonomy and feel supported by their manager.

Balancing Job Demands and Resources

To maintain high levels of engagement while avoiding burnout, organizations must carefully balance job demands and job resources:

- Reducing Excessive Job Demands: Managers should monitor workload distribution, time pressures, and emotional demands to prevent employees from feeling overwhelmed. Providing clear job descriptions and managing role expectations can also help reduce stress.

- Enhancing Job Resources: Investing in job resources, such as leadership development, employee support systems, career advancement opportunities, and a positive organizational culture, is essential for fostering engagement. Organizations that provide these resources help employees meet challenges, feel empowered, and maintain motivation over the long term.

The JD-R Model emphasizes that the dynamic interaction between job demands and resources determines both employee well-being and engagement. By managing this balance effectively, organizations can mitigate the risks of burnout while maximizing employee performance and engagement.

In summary, the Job Demands-Resources Model offers a comprehensive framework for understanding how the demands placed on employees and the resources available to them influence both burnout and engagement. It underscores the importance of not only managing work-related stress but also enhancing the factors that contribute to employee motivation and satisfaction. Organizations that prioritize a balance between job demands and resources are more likely to foster a resilient, engaged workforce that drives sustainable success.

Here's a typical diagram of the Job Demands-Resources (JD-R) Model, often found in academic literature on employee engagement:

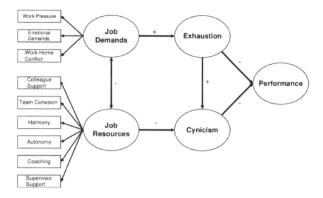

Explanation

Job Demands: These are stressors or pressures that require effort from employees. High demands can lead to stress and burnout if not balanced with adequate resources.

Stress and Burnout: Excessive job demands can result in stress and burnout, negatively impacting employee well-being and job satisfaction.

Employee Engagement: Engaged employees experience higher levels of emotional commitment, job satisfaction, and motivation.

Job Resources: These are supportive factors that help employees manage job demands and enhance their ability to achieve goals. They include things like autonomy, social support, and feedback.

Enhanced Employee Engagement: Adequate job resources can counterbalance high job demands, leading to improved employee engagement, motivation, and job satisfaction.

Part 3: Factors Influencing Employee Engagement

Employee engagement is shaped by a variety of factors that affect how individuals feel about their work, their colleagues, and the organization as a whole. These factors can either enhance or undermine engagement, and they are often interconnected. Understanding the key drivers of engagement helps organizations create an environment that fosters commitment, motivation, and performance.

Leadership and Management Style

Leadership plays a pivotal role in shaping employee engagement. The way leaders and managers interact with employees, make decisions, and set the tone for the organization influences the overall work environment.

Transformational Leadership: Leaders who inspire and motivate employees by sharing a compelling vision and encouraging innovation tend to drive higher engagement. Transformational leaders build trust, empower their teams, and create a sense of purpose, which fosters commitment.

Supportive Management: Managers who offer regular feedback, recognize employee efforts, and provide the necessary support help employees feel valued and engaged. A management style that emphasizes coaching and development, rather than control, is more likely to enhance engagement.

Consistency and Fairness: Leaders who are transparent, fair, and consistent in their actions build trust, which is essential for fostering employee engagement. Employees are more likely to stay engaged when they believe leadership acts in their best interest.

Organizational Culture

The culture of an organization is a reflection of its values, beliefs, and norms, and it plays a critical role in influencing employee engagement. A positive, inclusive, and dynamic culture enhances the likelihood that employees will be engaged and committed.

Values Alignment: When employees feel that the organizational culture aligns with their personal values, they are more likely to feel connected and engaged. A strong, mission-driven culture helps employees see how their work contributes to the larger goals of the organization.

Inclusive Culture: Organizations that promote diversity, equity, and inclusion create environments where all employees feel respected and valued. Inclusivity fosters a sense of belonging, which is crucial for engagement.

Collaboration and Openness: A culture that encourages collaboration, open communication, and teamwork creates a supportive environment in which employees feel engaged and invested in collective success.

Communication Practices

Effective communication is essential for maintaining engagement, as it ensures that employees are informed, involved, and connected with the organization's goals.

Transparency: Open and transparent communication from leadership helps employees understand organizational decisions, changes, and priorities. When well-informed, employees are more likely to trust leadership and stay engaged.

Two-Way Communication: Employees who feel that their voices are heard are more likely to be engaged. Organizations should promote two-way communication channels, such as feedback systems, town hall meetings, and employee surveys, to encourage dialogue between employees and management.

Clarity of Expectations: Clear communication of roles, responsibilities, and performance expectations helps employees understand their contribution to the organization. When employees clearly understand what is expected of them, they feel more confident and engaged in their work.

Job Design

The design of jobs, including the nature of tasks, responsibilities, and the degree of autonomy, significantly affects employee engagement. Well-designed jobs provide opportunities for meaningful work and personal growth.

Autonomy: Jobs that allow employees a degree of autonomy, or control over how they perform their tasks, are more likely to engage them. Employees who have the freedom to make decisions about their work feel empowered and responsible for their success.

Variety and Challenge: Job roles that offer variety and challenge prevent boredom and stagnation. Engaging employees with diverse tasks and opportunities for problem-solving enhances their interest and investment in their work.

Task Significance: When employees understand the impact of their work on the organization, customers, or society, they are more likely to feel engaged. Knowing that their work has purpose and meaning is a strong motivator.

Recognition and Rewards

Recognition and rewards are important drivers of employee engagement, as they reinforce positive behaviors and show employees that their contributions are valued.

Recognition of Efforts: Employees who receive regular recognition for their hard work and achievements are more likely to remain engaged. Recognition can come in various forms, including verbal praise, formal awards, or public acknowledgment of accomplishments.

Fair and Meaningful Rewards: Compensation, bonuses, and other rewards that are perceived as fair and aligned with employee contributions help maintain engagement. Non-monetary rewards, such as additional time off, professional development opportunities, or flexible work arrangements, also contribute to a sense of appreciation.

Peer Recognition: In addition to recognition from managers, acknowledgment from peers can have a strong impact on engagement. Peer-to-peer recognition fosters a sense of camaraderie and reinforces positive relationships within teams.

Work-Life Balance

Maintaining a healthy work-life balance is a key factor in sustaining employee engagement. When employees feel they can manage their personal and professional lives effectively, they are more likely to remain motivated and productive.

Flexible Work Options: Offering flexibility in work hours, remote work opportunities, or compressed workweeks can help employees balance their personal responsibilities and reduce stress. Employees who have control over their schedules are often more engaged.

Workload Management: Organizations that manage workloads effectively and prevent employee burnout contribute to higher levels of engagement. Overworking employees can lead to stress and disengagement, while a reasonable workload encourages sustained motivation.

Supportive Policies: Policies such as parental leave, health and wellness programs, and mental health support contribute to a better work-life balance and show that the organization cares about employee well-being.

Professional Growth and Development Opportunities

Opportunities for career growth and personal development are critical for engaging employees over the long term. Employees who feel they are progressing and developing new skills are more likely to remain committed to their organization.

Training and Development: Providing access to training programs, workshops, and skill development initiatives helps employees grow professionally. Employees who are learning and improving their skills are more motivated to apply their knowledge and contribute to the organization's success.

Career Pathing: Clear opportunities for career advancement and promotion help employees envision a future with the organization. When employees understand how they can grow within the company, they are more likely to be engaged and invested in their long-term success.

Mentorship and Coaching: Offering mentorship and coaching programs creates a supportive environment for growth. Employees who receive guidance from experienced colleagues feel more confident and are more engaged in their personal and professional development.

In conclusion, employee engagement is influenced by a range of factors, from leadership style and organizational culture to job design and professional growth opportunities. Organizations that focus on creating an environment that supports these factors are more likely to build a highly engaged, motivated, and productive workforce.

Part 4: Measuring Employee Engagement

Measuring employee engagement is essential for understanding an organization's overall morale and motivation. By using both quantitative and qualitative methods, organizations can assess the factors that influence engagement, identify areas for improvement, and implement strategies to enhance employee satisfaction and productivity.

Employee Engagement Surveys

Surveys are one of the most widely used tools for measuring employee engagement. They provide structured data on employees' feelings about their work, the organization, and overall engagement. Two common types of surveys include:

Gallup Q12 Survey

The Gallup Q12 Survey is one of the most recognized tools for measuring employee engagement. It consists of 12 questions that assess various aspects of employee engagement, such as recognition, opportunities for growth, and relationships with coworkers and managers. The questions are designed to capture the core elements that drive engagement:

Clear Expectations: Do employees know what is expected of them at work?

Opportunities to Excel: Are employees allowed to do what they do best every day?

Feedback and Recognition: Do employees regularly receive recognition for their work?

Development and Growth: Do employees have opportunities to learn and grow within the organization?

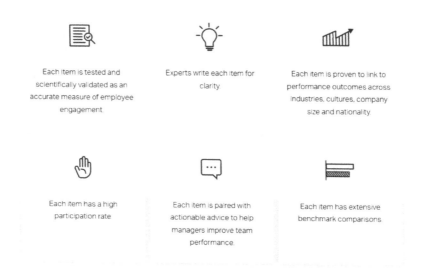

The Gallup Q12 Survey has been widely validated and used by organizations globally to gain insights into employee engagement and to benchmark against industry standards.

Custom Surveys

Custom surveys are tailored to the specific needs and goals of an organization. These surveys can include questions relevant to the company's unique culture, leadership style, or industry. Custom surveys allow organizations to focus on particular areas of interest, such as work-life balance, collaboration, or job satisfaction.

Flexibility: Custom surveys can be adjusted based on the evolving needs of the organization.

Specific Insights: By designing questions tailored to specific challenges or objectives, custom surveys can provide more in-depth insights into factors influencing engagement.

Both standardized and custom surveys are valuable tools for collecting quantitative data on employee engagement and tracking progress over time.

4.1. Key Metrics

In addition to surveys, several key metrics help organizations gauge employee engagement and assess the impact on business outcomes. These metrics provide insights into the overall health of the workforce.

Employee Net Promoter Score (eNPS)

The Employee Net Promoter Score (eNPS) is a popular employee loyalty and engagement measure. It is based on a single question: "On a scale of 0-10, how likely are you to recommend this organization as a great place to work?"

Promoters (9-10): Employees who are highly engaged and would recommend the organization.

Passives (7-8): Employees who are satisfied but not fully engaged.

Detractors (0-6): Disengaged Employees who are unlikely to recommend the organization.

The eNPS is calculated by subtracting the percentage of detractors from the percentage of promoters. A higher eNPS indicates stronger engagement and employee loyalty. It is an easy-to-administer tool and offers a quick snapshot of employee sentiment.

Turnover and Retention Rates

Turnover and retention rates are key indicators of employee engagement. High turnover, especially among top performers or in critical roles, may indicate disengagement or dissatisfaction within the workforce.

Turnover Rate: The percentage of employees who leave the organization within a given time period.

Retention Rate: The percentage of employees who remain with the organization over a specific period.

Tracking these metrics helps organizations understand if disengagement is leading to increased turnover, and whether strategies need to be implemented to improve retention.

Absenteeism

[An] important metric in understanding employee engagement. Frequent or unexplained [absences] can be a sign of low engagement, job dissatisfaction, or even burnout.

Patterns: Monitoring absenteeism rates and patterns can provide insights into employee well-being. High levels of absenteeism may indicate widespread disengagement or workplace [issues].

Organizations can use absenteeism data to address root causes, such as excessive [workload or poor] work-life balance, to re-engage employees.

[Surv]eys

[Empl]oyee

[While met]rics provide valuable quantitative data, qualitative methods offer deeper [understandin]g reasons for engagement or disengagement. These methods give employees [a chance to share t]heir thoughts and feelings in a more nuanced way.

Focus Groups

Focus groups involve gathering small groups of employees to discuss their experiences and perceptions about the workplace in an open and candid manner. These discussions allow organizations to gain deeper insights into specific engagement drivers and identify areas for improvement.

In-Depth Feedback: Focus groups encourage employees to share their experiences, providing qualitative insights into engagement challenges and opportunities.

Collaborative Solutions: Employees often share ideas and suggestions for improving engagement during focus group sessions, fostering a collaborative approach to enhancing the work environment.

Focus groups are especially useful for exploring issues that may not be easily captured through surveys, such as organizational culture or communication practices.

One-on-One Interviews

One-on-one interviews with employees provide an opportunity for more personalized and confidential feedback. These interviews allow for in-depth exploration of individual experiences, challenges, and perspectives on engagement.

Personalized Insights: Interviews provide detailed, individualized insights into what drives engagement for specific employees. Managers can use this information to tailor engagement strategies.

Addressing Sensitive Issues: Employees may feel more comfortable discussing sensitive topics one-on-one, making interviews a valuable tool for uncovering deeper engagement issues.

Qualitative methods, such as interviews and focus groups, complement quantitative surveys and metrics by providing richer, more detailed insights into employee engagement.

In conclusion, a comprehensive approach to measuring employee engagement includes both quantitative and qualitative methods. Surveys and key metrics provide data-driven insights, while qualitative methods help explore the underlying factors that influence engagement. By consistently measuring and analyzing employee engagement, organizations can take targeted actions to improve morale, reduce turnover, and create a more engaged and productive workforce.

Part 5: Strategies for Enhancing Employee Engagement

Enhancing employee engagement requires a multifaceted approach that addresses various aspects of the work environment and organizational culture. Organizations can create a more engaged and motivated workforce by implementing strategies that focus on leadership, work environment, empowerment, recognition, career development, and work-life integration.

Leadership Development

Effective leadership is crucial for fostering employee engagement. Developing leaders who can inspire, support, and guide their teams is essential for creating an engaged workforce.

Leadership Training: Provide leaders with training programs that focus on key skills such as emotional intelligence, communication, and coaching. Equip them with tools and techniques to motivate and engage their teams.

Mentoring and Coaching: Establish mentoring and coaching programs to help leaders develop their skills and provide guidance. Experienced leaders can share best practices and support new or emerging leaders.

Leadership Feedback: Implement 360-degree feedback processes to give leaders various perspectives on their performance. Use this feedback to guide leadership development efforts and address areas for improvement.

Effective leaders inspire and motivate their teams, create a positive work environment, and drive employee engagement through their actions and decisions.

Creating a Positive Work Environment

A positive work environment is foundational for employee engagement. Organizations should focus on creating a supportive and inclusive culture that fosters trust, collaboration, and well-being.

Building Trust and Transparency

Open Communication: Foster open and honest communication between employees and management. Share information about organizational goals, changes, and decisions transparently to build trust.

Consistency and Integrity: Ensure that policies and practices are applied consistently and fairly. Leaders should act with integrity and demonstrate ethical behavior to build a culture of trust.

Employee Involvement: Involve employees in decision-making processes and seek their input on important matters. When employees feel they have a voice in shaping the organization, trust and engagement increase.

Encouraging Collaboration

Team Building Activities: Organize team-building activities and events to strengthen relationships and improve collaboration among employees. Foster a sense of camaraderie and teamwork.

Collaborative Tools: Implement tools and technologies that facilitate collaboration, such as project management software, communication platforms, and shared workspaces.

Cross-Functional Projects: Encourage cross-functional projects and teams to promote interaction and cooperation across different departments. Collaborative projects help employees build relationships and understand diverse perspectives.

Creating a positive work environment that emphasizes trust, transparency, and collaboration enhances employee engagement and satisfaction.

5.1. Empowering Employees

Empowering employees involves giving them the autonomy and authority to make decisions and take ownership of their work. This approach fosters a sense of responsibility and increases engagement.

Encouraging Autonomy

Flexible Work Arrangements: Offer flexible work options, such as remote work or flexible hours, to allow employees to manage their work in a way that suits their personal preferences and needs.

Decision-Making Authority: Delegate decision-making authority to employees, allowing them to take ownership of their tasks and projects. Empower employees to solve problems and make decisions related to their work.

Encouraging Innovation: Support a culture of innovation by encouraging employees to propose and implement new ideas. Provide resources and support for experimentation and creativity.

Enabling Decision-Making

Clear Expectations: Set clear expectations and goals to guide employees in their decision-making. Provide the necessary information and context to help employees make informed choices.

Training and Support: Offer training and resources to help employees develop the skills and confidence needed for effective decision-making. Provide ongoing support and guidance as needed.

Feedback and Recognition: Provide regular feedback and recognition for effective decision-making. Acknowledge and reward employees for their contributions and successful outcomes.

Empowering employees by providing autonomy and decision-making authority increases engagement and fosters a sense of ownership and responsibility.

Recognizing and Rewarding Employees

Recognition and rewards are powerful tools for motivating and engaging employees. Organizations can reinforce positive behaviors and enhance satisfaction by acknowledging and rewarding employees for their contributions.

Regular Recognition: Implement a system for regular recognition of employee achievements, both big and small. Recognize employees publicly, privately, or through formal award programs.

Tailored Rewards: Offer a variety of rewards that align with employee preferences and interests. This could include monetary rewards, additional time off, or personalized gifts.

Peer Recognition: Encourage peer-to-peer recognition programs where employees can acknowledge and appreciate each other's contributions. This fosters a culture of appreciation and reinforces positive relationships.

Recognition and rewards that are timely, specific, and aligned with employee preferences enhance engagement and motivate employees to continue contributing to the organization.

5.2. Career Development and Growth

Providing opportunities for career development and growth is essential for maintaining employee engagement. Employees who see a clear path for advancement are more likely to be motivated and committed.

Career Pathing: Develop clear career paths and progression opportunities within the organization. Provide employees with a roadmap for advancement and the skills required for different roles.

Training and Development: Invest in training and development programs that help employees build new skills and advance their careers. Offer workshops, seminars, and online courses to support continuous learning.

Mentorship Programs: Establish mentorship programs that pair employees with experienced mentors who can provide guidance, support, and career advice.

Career development opportunities that are aligned with employees' goals and aspirations enhance engagement and retention by showing that the organization is invested in their growth.

Supporting Work-Life Integration

Supporting work-life integration helps employees balance their professional and personal lives, which is crucial for maintaining engagement and overall well-being.

Flexible Work Policies: Implement flexible work policies that allow employees to manage their work schedules and locations according to their needs. Options such as remote work, flexible hours, and compressed workweeks can support work-life integration.

Wellness Programs: Offer wellness programs that promote physical and mental health. This can include fitness classes, counseling services, and stress management resources.

Work-Life Resources: Provide resources and support for employees to manage personal responsibilities, such as childcare assistance, parental leave, and employee assistance programs.

Supporting work-life integration demonstrates that the organization values employees' well-being and fosters a more engaged and satisfied workforce.

In conclusion, enhancing employee engagement involves a comprehensive approach that addresses leadership development, work environment, empowerment, recognition, career growth, and work-life integration. By implementing these strategies, organizations can create a supportive and motivating work environment that drives higher engagement, performance, and satisfaction levels.

5.3. Role of Technology in Managing Engagement

Technology plays a critical role in managing and enhancing employee engagement by providing tools and platforms that facilitate communication, collaboration, and data analysis. Leveraging technology helps organizations gather insights, streamline processes, and create a more connected and engaged workforce.

Employee Engagement Platforms

Employee engagement platforms are specialized software solutions designed to measure, manage, and improve employee engagement. These platforms offer various features to support engagement strategies, from surveys and feedback collection to recognition and development tools.

Examples of Tools and Software

Survey Tools: Platforms like SurveyMonkey, Qualtrics, and Culture Amp enable organizations to conduct regular engagement surveys, gather feedback, and analyze employee sentiment. These tools often include pre-built survey templates, customization options, and reporting features.

Engagement and Recognition Platforms: Officevibe, Bonusly, and 15Five offer ongoing employee feedback, recognition, and engagement solutions. These platforms allow employees to give and receive recognition, provide feedback, and track engagement metrics in real-time.

Performance Management Systems: Lattice, Trakstar, and Reflektive integrate performance management with engagement tracking. These systems provide tools for goal setting, performance reviews, and development planning while also measuring engagement levels.

Internal Communication Tools: Platforms like Slack, Microsoft Teams, and Yammer facilitate team communication and collaboration. They support engagement by enabling real-time messaging, file sharing, and team collaboration.

Employee engagement platforms help organizations collect and analyze data, recognize achievements, and foster a culture of continuous feedback and improvement.

Analytics and Data-Driven Insights

Analytics and data-driven insights play a crucial role in understanding and improving employee engagement. Organizations can identify trends, diagnose issues, and make informed decisions to enhance engagement strategies by analyzing data.

Engagement Metrics Analysis: Analyzing metrics such as survey results, eNPS scores, turnover rates, and absenteeism can provide insights into employee engagement levels and areas for improvement. Data analysis helps identify patterns and correlations that inform engagement strategies.

Predictive Analytics: Predictive analytics tools use historical data and statistical models to forecast future engagement trends and potential issues. By anticipating problems before they arise, organizations can take proactive measures to address engagement challenges.

Customized Dashboards: Advanced analytics platforms offer customizable dashboards that allow managers and HR professionals to track engagement metrics in real-time. These dashboards provide visualizations of key data points and trends, making it easier to monitor and respond to engagement levels.

Sentiment Analysis: Sentiment analysis tools analyze employee feedback, social media posts, and other text data to gauge overall sentiment and identify areas of concern. These tools use natural language processing (NLP) and machine learning to interpret and categorize employee sentiments.

Data-driven insights enable organizations to make evidence-based decisions, tailor engagement initiatives, and measure the impact of their strategies.

5.4. Remote Work and Digital Collaboration Tools

Remote work and digital collaboration tools are essential for employee engagement, especially in hybrid or remote work environments. These tools help employees stay connected, collaborate effectively, and remain engaged regardless of their physical location.

Virtual Meeting Platforms: Tools like Zoom, Microsoft Teams, and Google Meet facilitate virtual meetings and video conferences. These platforms support face-to-face interactions, team collaboration, and effective communication, which are crucial for maintaining engagement in remote settings.

Project Management Software: Platforms such as Asana, Trello, and Monday.com help teams manage projects, track progress, and coordinate tasks. These tools enhance transparency, accountability, and collaboration, contributing to higher engagement levels.

Employee Engagement Apps: Mobile apps like Workforce and Jostle provide on-the-go access to engagement resources, company news, and communication channels. These apps keep remote employees informed and connected with the organization.

Digital Feedback and Recognition: Digital feedback and recognition tools, such as Kudos and Reward Gateway, enable employees to give and receive feedback and recognition in real time. These tools help sustain a culture of appreciation and motivation, even in virtual environments.

By integrating remote work and collaboration tools into daily operations, organizations can ensure that employees remain engaged, connected, and productive, regardless of their work location.

In conclusion, technology plays a vital role in managing employee engagement by providing platforms for feedback, recognition, and communication and tools for data analysis and remote collaboration. By leveraging these technological advancements, organizations can enhance their engagement strategies, gain valuable insights, and create a more connected and motivated workforce.

Part 6: Challenges in Managing Employee Engagement

Managing employee engagement presents several challenges that organizations must navigate to build a committed and motivated workforce. These challenges include addressing global and cultural differences, managing engagement in hybrid work environments, dealing with resistance to change, and balancing engagement with performance.

Global and Cultural Differences

Global and cultural differences can impact how engagement is perceived and managed across diverse teams and regions. Organizations operating in multiple countries or with a culturally diverse workforce may face unique challenges in fostering engagement.

Varied Expectations: Different cultures have varying expectations regarding work, leadership, and communication. Understanding and accommodating these differences is crucial for creating engagement strategies that resonate with all employees.

Communication Barriers: Language differences and communication styles can lead to misunderstandings and reduce the effectiveness of engagement initiatives. Ensuring clear, culturally sensitive communication is essential.

Cultural Norms: Engagement practices that work in one cultural context may not be effective in another. For example, recognition and rewards might be perceived differently across cultures, requiring tailored approaches to meet diverse expectations.

Organizations must develop strategies that respect and incorporate cultural differences to enhance engagement across global teams.

Managing Engagement in a Hybrid Workforce

Managing engagement in a hybrid workforce—where employees work both remotely and in the office—presents unique challenges. Balancing the needs of remote and on-site employees is essential for maintaining engagement levels across the organization.

Maintaining Connection: Ensuring that remote employees feel as connected and valued as those in the office can be challenging. Strategies must be implemented to foster inclusivity and equal participation for all team members.

Consistent Communication: Effective communication is crucial for keeping both remote and on-site employees informed and engaged. Organizations need to adopt communication tools and practices that work well in a hybrid environment.

Equitable Access: Providing equal access to opportunities, resources, and recognition for all employees, regardless of their work location, is essential. Ensuring that remote employees have the same opportunities for growth and development as their in-office counterparts helps maintain engagement.

Addressing these challenges requires thoughtful planning and the implementation of inclusive practices that support engagement across both remote and on-site teams.

Dealing with Resistance to Change

Resistance to change can hinder efforts to improve employee engagement, especially when introducing new initiatives, processes, or technologies. Overcoming resistance is key to successfully implementing engagement strategies.

Understanding Concerns: Identifying and addressing the reasons behind resistance is crucial. Employees may resist change due to fear of the unknown, perceived threats to job security, or a lack of trust in leadership.

Effective Communication: Clear and transparent communication about the reasons for change and its benefits can help mitigate resistance. Involving employees in the change process and seeking their input can also reduce opposition.

Training and Support: Providing training and support to help employees adapt to new changes is essential. Ensuring that employees have the resources and guidance needed to navigate transitions helps build confidence and reduce resistance.

Managing resistance effectively requires a proactive approach that involves listening to employees, communicating transparently, and providing support throughout the change process.

Balancing Engagement with Performance

Balancing engagement with performance involves ensuring that efforts to boost engagement do not negatively impact productivity or performance. Organizations need to find a balance between fostering a positive work environment and achieving high performance standards.

Performance Metrics: Developing and implementing performance metrics that align with engagement goals is important. Metrics should be designed to measure both engagement and productivity, providing a comprehensive view of employee performance.

Avoiding Overemphasis: While engagement is important, it should not come at the expense of performance. Striking the right balance involves setting clear expectations and ensuring that engagement initiatives support rather than detract from performance goals.

Continuous Feedback: Providing continuous feedback helps employees understand how their engagement and performance are interconnected. Regular check-ins and performance reviews can help identify and address any issues related to engagement and productivity.

Organizations must carefully manage engagement initiatives to ensure they enhance rather than hinder performance, creating a work environment that supports high engagement and high productivity.

In summary, managing employee engagement involves navigating challenges related to global and cultural differences, hybrid work environments, resistance to change, and balancing engagement with performance. Organizations can create a more engaged and productive workforce by addressing these challenges with thoughtful strategies and practices.

Part 7: Case Studies

Case studies provide valuable insights into how different organizations approach employee engagement, including both successful programs and instances where efforts fell short. Analyzing these real-world examples helps in understanding effective strategies and learning from mistakes.

Success Stories of Engagement Programs**

Examining success stories of engagement programs highlights effective strategies and practices that organizations have implemented to boost employee engagement and achieve positive outcomes.

Case Study 1: Google

Google is renowned for its innovative approach to employee engagement. The company has implemented several successful initiatives that foster a highly engaged workforce:

Employee Perks and Benefits: Google offers a wide range of employee perks, including on-site childcare, fitness centers, and free meals. These benefits contribute to a positive work environment and support work-life balance.

Open Communication: Google encourages open communication through regular town hall meetings and feedback sessions. Employees have access to leadership and can voice their opinions and ideas.

Career Development: Google invests heavily in employee development, offering various training programs, mentorship opportunities, and career growth initiatives. The company's commitment to personal and professional growth enhances employee engagement and satisfaction.

Results: Google consistently ranks as one of the best places to work due to its effective engagement strategies. The company has high employee retention rates and is known for its innovative and collaborative work culture.

Case Study 2: Salesforce

Salesforce has also achieved notable success in employee engagement through its focus on culture and values:

Ohana Culture: Salesforce's "Ohana" culture emphasizes family-like support and inclusivity. The company prioritizes employee well-being and fosters a strong sense of community and belonging.

Recognition Programs: Salesforce has implemented various recognition programs, including peer-to-peer recognition and annual awards, to celebrate employee achievements and contributions.

Community Involvement: Salesforce encourages employees to participate in community service and charitable activities. The company's commitment to social responsibility enhances employee engagement and morale.

Results: Salesforce has been recognized for its outstanding workplace culture and employee satisfaction. The company's engagement initiatives contribute to its strong performance and high levels of employee loyalty.

Failure to Engage: Lessons Learned

Analyzing cases where engagement efforts have failed provides important lessons for improving future initiatives and avoiding common pitfalls.

Case Study 1: Yahoo

Yahoo faced challenges with employee engagement during its period of significant restructuring:

Communication Issues: Yahoo struggled with communication during its restructuring phase. Frequent changes in leadership and unclear messaging led to confusion and disengagement among employees.

Workplace Flexibility: Yahoo's decision to eliminate remote work options was met with resistance. Employees valued the flexibility of working from home, and the removal of this option negatively impacted engagement and morale.

Leadership Changes: Frequent changes in leadership created instability and uncertainty. Employees felt disconnected from the company's vision and goals, leading to decreased engagement.

Lessons Learned: Effective communication and consistency in leadership are crucial for maintaining employee engagement during periods of change. Providing flexibility and considering employee preferences can also impact engagement levels.

Case Study 2: Sears

Sears experienced difficulties with employee engagement as it faced financial and operational challenges:

Lack of Investment in Employee Development: Sears reduced its investment in employee training and development, leading to a lack of career growth opportunities and declining employee morale.

Inconsistent Recognition: The company's recognition programs were perceived as inconsistent and unfair. Employees felt undervalued and unappreciated, which negatively impacted their engagement and commitment.

Resistance to Change: Sears struggled to implement changes effectively, leading to resistance from employees who were skeptical about the company's direction and future prospects.

Lessons Learned: Investing in employee development and implementing fair and consistent recognition programs are vital for maintaining engagement. Managing change effectively and addressing employee concerns can help mitigate resistance and enhance engagement.

In summary, success stories of engagement programs demonstrate the positive impact of effective strategies, such as offering comprehensive benefits, fostering open communication, and investing in employee development. Conversely, failures highlight the importance of clear communication, flexibility, and consistency in engagement efforts. By learning from these case studies, organizations can refine their engagement strategies and create more effective and sustainable programs.

Part 9: Future Trends in Employee Engagement

As the workplace evolves, so do the trends and strategies related to employee engagement. Understanding these future trends helps organizations stay ahead and adapt their engagement practices to meet emerging needs and expectations.

AI and Machine Learning in Engagement Strategies

AI and machine learning are increasingly being integrated into employee engagement strategies to enhance personalization, predict trends, and streamline processes.

Predictive Analytics: AI can analyze employee data to predict engagement trends, identify potential issues before they become critical, and recommend targeted interventions. For example, AI algorithms can analyze survey responses and other data to forecast turnover risks and suggest strategies to improve retention.

Personalized Engagement: Machine learning algorithms can tailor engagement initiatives to individual employee preferences and needs. For instance, AI-powered platforms can recommend personalized development opportunities, recognition methods, or communication approaches based on employee behavior and feedback.

Chatbots and Virtual Assistants: AI-driven chatbots and virtual assistants can facilitate real-time communication, provide instant feedback, and answer employee queries about engagement programs, policies, and benefits. This technology helps improve accessibility and responsiveness in engagement management.

The use of AI and machine learning in engagement strategies enhances the ability to analyze data, personalize experiences, and proactively address engagement challenges.

The Role of Purpose and Corporate Social Responsibility (CSR)

Purpose and corporate social responsibility (CSR) are becoming increasingly important in shaping employee engagement. Employees are seeking more than just financial rewards; they want to work for organizations that align with their values and contribute positively to society.

Purpose-Driven Work: Employees are increasingly motivated by a sense of purpose and alignment with their personal values. Organizations that clearly articulate their mission and demonstrate how employees' work contributes to a greater good tend to have higher engagement levels.

CSR Initiatives: Effective CSR programs that focus on social, environmental, and ethical issues can boost employee engagement by fostering a sense of pride and commitment. Employees are more engaged when they feel their employer is making a positive impact on society and the environment.

Employee Involvement in CSR: Involving employees in CSR activities and decision-making can enhance engagement by giving them opportunities to contribute to meaningful causes. Programs that encourage volunteerism and community involvement strengthen employees' connection to the organization.

Organizations that embrace purpose and CSR as central elements of their engagement strategies are likely to attract and retain employees who are passionate about making a difference.

The Impact of Generational Shifts

Generational shifts are influencing employee engagement strategies as organizations adapt to the preferences and expectations of a multi-generational workforce.

Millennials and Gen Z: Younger generations, such as Millennials and Gen Z, prioritize work-life balance, flexibility, and career development. Engagement strategies that address these preferences—such as offering remote work options, flexible schedules, and opportunities for growth—are essential for attracting and retaining younger employees.

Diverse Work Expectations: Different generations have varying expectations regarding workplace culture, communication, and recognition. Organizations need to adopt diverse engagement practices that cater to the needs of all generational groups while fostering intergenerational collaboration.

Technology Integration: Younger generations are more comfortable with technology and expect digital communication, feedback, and development solutions. Integrating advanced technology, such as mobile apps and digital platforms, into engagement strategies can enhance the experience for tech-savvy employees.

Understanding and addressing the preferences of different generations helps organizations create inclusive engagement strategies that resonate with a diverse workforce.

In conclusion, future trends in employee engagement are shaped by advancements in technology, the growing importance of purpose and CSR, and the impact of generational shifts. Organizations can develop more effective and forward-looking engagement strategies by leveraging AI and machine learning, embracing purpose-driven initiatives, and adapting to the expectations of a multi-generational workforce.

In conclusion, effective management of employee engagement is crucial for fostering a motivated and productive workforce. As we have explored, a comprehensive approach to engagement involves understanding key theories, recognizing influencing factors, implementing effective measurement and enhancement strategies, and addressing challenges.

Recap of Key Points

Definition and Importance: Employee engagement refers to employees' emotional commitment and enthusiasm towards their work and organization. It is vital for organizational success as it drives performance, productivity, and employee satisfaction.

Theories of Engagement: Key theories such as the Engagement Pyramid, Self-Determination Theory, and the Job Demands-Resources Model offer valuable frameworks for understanding and enhancing engagement.

Influencing Factors: Leadership, organizational culture, communication, job design, recognition, work-life balance, and professional development significantly impact employee engagement.

Measurement: Effective measurement of engagement involves using surveys, key metrics like eNPS, turnover rates, absenteeism, and qualitative methods such as focus groups and interviews.

Enhancement Strategies: Successful engagement strategies include leadership development, creating a positive work environment, empowering employees, recognizing and rewarding contributions, supporting career growth, and facilitating work-life integration.

Technology: Advances in AI, machine learning, and digital tools are transforming engagement management by offering personalized insights, enhancing communication, and supporting remote work.

Challenges: Managing engagement involves addressing global and cultural differences, adapting to hybrid work environments, overcoming resistance to change, and balancing engagement with performance.

Case Studies: Successful examples from companies like Google and Salesforce highlight effective engagement practices, while failures from organizations like Yahoo and Sears provide lessons on avoiding common pitfalls.

The Importance of Continuous Engagement Management

Continuous engagement management is essential for maintaining a motivated and high-performing workforce. Engagement is not a one-time effort but an ongoing process that requires regular attention and adaptation. Organizations must:

Monitor and Adapt: Regularly assess engagement levels and adapt strategies based on feedback, data, and changing circumstances. This involves staying attuned to employee needs and industry trends.

Foster a Culture of Engagement: Create a culture where engagement is a core value and where employees feel continuously supported, recognized, and valued.

Innovate and Evolve: Embrace new technologies, methodologies, and practices to keep engagement strategies fresh and relevant. Innovation helps address emerging challenges and opportunities in the evolving workplace.

Final Thoughts on Future Engagement Strategies

Looking ahead, future engagement strategies will need to adapt to ongoing changes in technology, workforce demographics, and organizational priorities. Key considerations for the future include:

Embracing Technological Advancements: Leverage AI, machine learning, and digital tools to enhance personalization, predictive analytics, and remote work engagement.

Aligning with Purpose and CSR: Integrate purpose-driven initiatives and CSR efforts into engagement strategies to resonate with employees' values and contribute to societal impact.

Adapting to Generational Shifts: Address a multi-generational workforce's diverse needs and expectations by offering flexible, inclusive, and technology-driven engagement solutions.

Organizations can build a resilient and engaged workforce that drives long-term success and growth by staying proactive and responsive to these trends.

Student Takeaway:

Managing employee engagement is crucial for fostering a productive and motivated workforce. Engaged employees are more committed, creative, and contribute positively. Leaders must prioritize open communication, recognize achievements, and provide growth opportunities to enhance engagement. A supportive work environment that promotes work-life balance and inclusivity also plays a key role. Effective leadership is essential for inspiring and empowering employees, while regular assessment of engagement levels helps identify areas for improvement. Ultimately, engaged employees drive better organizational performance and create a more positive, collaborative workplace culture.

Glossary of Key Terms in Employee Engagement

I. Employee Engagement: The level of commitment, enthusiasm, and involvement employees have towards their organization and its goals, which impacts their motivation and job performance.

II. Job Satisfaction: The extent to which employees feel content with their job roles, responsibilities, and work environment, influencing their overall engagement and retention.

III. Motivation: The internal and external factors that drive employees to perform well, including personal goals, incentives, and recognition.

IV. Commitment: The emotional attachment and loyalty employees feel towards their organization, often reflected in their willingness to put in extra effort and stay with the company.

V. Employee Retention: The ability of an organization to keep its employees over time, often enhanced by high levels of engagement and job satisfaction.

VI. Workplace Culture: The shared values, beliefs, and practices that shape the work environment and influence employee behavior and engagement.

VII. Recognition and Rewards: The acknowledgment and appreciation of employees' contributions and achievements can enhance their engagement and motivation.

VIII. Feedback: Providing employees with information about their performance helps them understand how they can improve and feel more connected to their work.

IX. Career Development: Opportunities for employees to grow and advance within the organization, which can increase engagement by aligning personal career goals with organizational objectives.

X. Work-Life Balance: The ability to effectively manage work responsibilities alongside personal life, contributing to employee satisfaction and overall engagement.

XI. Employee Well-being: The overall health and happiness of employees, including mental, physical, and emotional aspects, which affect their engagement and productivity.

XII. Empowerment: Giving employees the authority and autonomy to make decisions and contribute ideas can boost their sense of ownership and engagement.

XIII. Team Collaboration: The effectiveness of employees working together towards common goals, which can enhance engagement through shared purpose and support.

XIV. Communication: The exchange of information between employees and management, including clarity of expectations and openness to feedback, which impacts engagement levels.

XV. Organizational Commitment: The degree to which employees feel aligned with and invested in the organization's goals and values, influencing their engagement level.

XVI. Employee Experience: The overall journey of employees within an organization, including recruitment, onboarding, development, and daily interactions, which affects engagement.

XVII. Engagement Surveys: Tools used to measure employees' attitudes, satisfaction, and levels of engagement, providing insights for improving workplace practices.

XVIII. Job Enrichment: Enhancing the quality of employees' job roles by adding variety, autonomy, and opportunities for skill development, which can increase engagement.

XIX. Leadership Effectiveness: The ability of leaders to inspire, motivate, and support their teams, significantly impacting employee engagement and organizational performance.

XX. Performance Management: The ongoing process of setting goals, providing feedback, and evaluating employee performance to support development and engagement.

Chapter 4: Leadership for Corporate Excellence

Part 1: Introduction

Leadership is the cornerstone of any thriving organization. It is the ability to influence and guide individuals or teams toward achieving common goals. In this chapter, we will explore the essential components of leadership, the different styles and theories that guide it, and its critical role in corporate excellence. Understanding these concepts will equip you with the knowledge to foster leadership skills in your HR role, shaping high performing teams and contributing to organizational success.

1.1. What is Leadership?

- Leadership can be defined as the art of influencing people to work toward the attainment of a common goal. It involves more than just giving directions or managing tasks—it's about inspiring individuals to perform beyond expectations. While leadership and management are often used interchangeably, there's a clear distinction.

- Leadership is focused on creating a vision and inspiring others to follow it. It involves setting direction, building relationships, and driving innovation.

- Management deals with administering and ensuring the effective execution of processes and systems already in place.

A good leader does both. They are visionaries who also manage resources effectively to achieve their goals.

1.2. Leadership Theories

Leadership is not a one size fits all concept. Over time, various theories have emerged to explain what makes an effective leader. Let's explore a few:

- ✓ **Trait Theory:** This theory suggests that leaders are born, not made. It emphasizes the importance of certain personality traits like confidence, decisiveness, and integrity. While this idea has its merits, modern theories recognize that leadership skills can be developed over time.

- ✓ **Behavioral Theories:** Instead of focusing on inherent traits, these theories examine what leaders do.

Ohio State Studies identified two key behaviors:

- Initiating Structure: Leaders clearly define tasks and roles.
- Consideration: Leaders show concern for their employees' well-being and create a supportive work environment.

Michigan Studies differentiated between:

- Production Oriented Leaders: Focus on getting the job done.
- Employee Oriented Leaders: Focus on building strong relationships with their team.

✓ **Contingency Theories:** These theories suggest that the effectiveness of a leader depends on the situation.

For example:

Fiedler's Model argues that leadership style should fit the situation, whether it's a task focused or relationship focused approach.

Path Goal Theory emphasizes the leader's role in clearing obstacles for employees so they can achieve their goals.

Situational Leadership suggests that leaders must adapt their style depending on their team's development level—ranging from directive to supportive.

1.3. Leadership Styles

Leadership styles can significantly impact how a team functions and achieves its goals. Some common styles include:

I. Autocratic Leadership: The leader makes decisions unilaterally, expecting followers to comply. This style can be effective for quick decision making but often stifles creativity and employee engagement.

II. Democratic Leadership: Here, the leader involves team members in decision making, fostering collaboration and enhancing morale.

III. Laissezfaire Leadership: This hands off approach works well with highly skilled teams, allowing individuals the freedom to manage their tasks. However, it can lead to a lack of direction if not properly managed.

IV. Transactional Leadership: This style is based on rewards and punishments to motivate performance. Leaders set clear goals, and employees are rewarded or penalized based on their ability to achieve those goals.

V. Transformational Leadership: Transformational leaders inspire their followers by creating a compelling vision for the future. They encourage employees to exceed their own expectations and achieve higher levels of performance. This style is often associated with successful change management in organizations.

VI. Servant Leadership: Servant leaders prioritize the needs of their team members and focus on their growth and well being. They believe that by serving their team, they will achieve better results. This style is particularly effective in organizations that value employee engagement and satisfaction.

VII. Authentic Leadership: Authentic leaders are genuine and transparent in their actions. They build trust through consistency, integrity, and ethical behavior, fostering a loyal and motivated team.

1.4. Leadership and Corporate Governance

Leadership plays a pivotal role in corporate governance, which refers to the mechanisms, processes, and relations by which corporations are controlled and directed. A strong leader not only drives organizational performance but also shapes its culture, ethical values, and decision making processes.

Corporate governance focuses on:

Ethical Leadership: Leaders set the tone for integrity and transparency within the company.

Corporate Culture: Leaders influence the development of a positive culture where employees feel valued and motivated.

Example: Satya Nadella, the CEO of Microsoft, transformed the company's culture by promoting a growth mindset, fostering collaboration, and focusing on customer centric innovation. His leadership reshaped Microsoft's trajectory, making it a global leader in cloud computing and AI technology.

Part 2: Leadership Development and Skills

2.1. Leadership Development Frameworks

Developing leadership skills is essential for both personal growth and organizational success. One popular model is the 702010 Model:

- 70% of leadership development comes from onthejob experiences, where leaders learn by facing real challenges.
- 20% comes from feedback and interactions, such as mentorship or peer discussions.
- 10% comes from formal education, including leadership training programs or courses.

HR departments play a critical role in nurturing future leaders by offering development opportunities and creating pathways for employees to grow.

2.2. Essential Leadership Skills

i. Leadership is more than just delegating tasks—it requires a variety of skills. The most effective leaders master several key abilities:

ii. Emotional Intelligence (EQ): Leaders with high EQ can manage their own emotions and understand those of their employees, creating a more empathetic and productive work environment.

iii. Communication Skills: Clear and effective communication ensures that everyone understands the organization's goals and their role in achieving them.

iv. Conflict Management: Leaders must mediate conflicts and foster a culture where disagreements are resolved constructively.

v. Delegation and Empowerment: By empowering employees and giving them autonomy, leaders build trust and enable higher levels of performance.

vi. DecisionMaking: Good leaders are decisive, but they also consider input from their team to make informed decisions.

2.3. Leadership in Different Contexts

Leadership styles and strategies may need to be adapted depending on the organization's size, goals, and market context.

Small vs. Large Organizations: In smaller organizations, leadership tends to be more hands-on, while larger organizations require leaders who can delegate effectively and manage complex hierarchies.

Global Leadership: Within multinational organizations, leaders encounter the formidable task of overseeing diverse teams across varying cultural and geographical contexts. Cross-cultural leadership demands a high level of cultural sensitivity, adaptability, and a broad-minded approach.

Ethical Leadership

Leaders should uphold ethical standards and act with integrity in all decisions

Transparency and accountability are crucial in ethical leadership practices

Innovation Leadership

Encourage a culture of innovation and creativity within the organization

Foster an environment where employees feel empowered to suggest new ideas and solutions

Transformational Leadership

Inspire and motivate employees to achieve their full potential

Lead by example and create a vision that aligns with the organization's goals and values.

Example: During a crisis, effective leaders exhibit calm, decisiveness, and compassion. Johnson & Johnson's handling of the Tylenol poisoning crisis is a textbook example of crisis management, where leadership's swift and transparent response helped restore public trust.

2.4. Role of HR in Leadership Development

HR professionals are pivotal in shaping future leaders by offering:

Succession Planning: Identifying and developing future leaders ensures business continuity.

Leadership Training Programs: Structured programs, workshops, and mentorship opportunities can help employees develop leadership skills.

Performance Appraisal Systems: HR uses these systems to assess leadership potential and identify areas for growth.

Part 3: Leadership and Organizational Performance

3.1. Corporate Excellence and Leadership

Leadership is directly tied to corporate excellence. Leaders drive performance by:

Setting a Clear Vision: A visionary leader paints a compelling picture of the future, aligning the team around a common goal.

Creating a High Performance Culture: Through strong leadership, organizations can cultivate a culture of accountability, innovation, and collaboration.

Example: Jeff Bezos' leadership at Amazon, where his long term vision of customer-centric innovation transformed the company from an online bookstore to a global e-commerce giant.

3.2. Strategic Leadership

Strategic leaders are responsible for formulating and implementing long term goals that align with the organization's vision. They focus on:

Creating a Strategic Vision: Leaders articulate the future direction of the company.

Executing Strategy: Leaders must ensure that the organization's resources and capabilities are aligned with its strategic goals.

A key part of strategic leadership is leading through change. John Kotter's 8Step Change Model outlines how leaders can guide their organizations through transformation, from creating a sense of urgency to anchoring new approaches into the culture.

3.3. Leadership and Innovation

Leaders play a vital role in fostering a culture of innovation by encouraging creativity, risktaking, and continuous learning.

Example: Steve Jobs at Apple focused on design and simplicity, driving the company to become one of the world's most innovative technology firms.

3.4. Measuring Leadership Effectiveness

To ensure that leadership efforts are driving performance, organizations use various methods to assess leadership effectiveness:

- Employee Engagement Surveys: High engagement often indicates robust leadership.
- 360-Degree Feedback: This process enables leaders to solicit feedback from their peers, subordinates, and supervisors, offering a comprehensive assessment of their leadership style and efficacy.

Leadership is the engine that drives corporate excellence. Whether through fostering innovation, guiding strategic change, or developing future leaders, the role of a leader is essential to the success of any organization. For HR professionals, understanding leadership theories, styles, and skills is critical to shaping an effective and high performing workforce. As the business environment becomes increasingly complex and dynamic, the need for agile, ethical, and visionary leadership will continue to grow.

3.5. Student Takeaway:

Students should grasp that leadership is crucial for organizational success and involves more than just management—it's about vision, inspiration, and effective resource use. Understanding various leadership theories, styles, and skills can help you develop effective leaders and drive high performance. Emphasize continuous learning and adaptability in leadership roles to foster innovation, ethical behavior, and strategic growth.

Glossary for Leadership for Corporate Excellence

I. Leadership: The process of influencing and guiding individuals or teams towards achieving a common goal, involving vision creation, relationship building, and driving innovation.

II. Management: The act of administering and executing tasks effectively, focusing on maintaining processes and systems already in place.

III. Trait Theory: A theory suggesting that effective leaders are born with certain personality traits like confidence and integrity, although modern views acknowledge leadership can be developed.

IV. Behavioral Theories: Leadership theories that focus on what leaders do rather than their traits, including key behaviors like initiating structure and showing consideration for employees.

V. Ohio State Studies: Identified two key leadership behaviors:

VI. - Initiating Structure: Defining tasks and roles.

VII. - Consideration: Showing concern for employee well-being and fostering a supportive environment.

VIII. Michigan Studies: Differentiated between:

IX. - Production-Oriented Leaders: Focus on completing tasks.

X. - Employee-Oriented Leaders: Focus on fostering relationships with their team.

XI. Contingency Theories: Suggest that leadership effectiveness depends on the situation or context, requiring leaders to adapt their style.

XII. Fiedler's Model: A contingency theory proposing that leadership style should match the situation, whether task-focused or relationship-focused.

XIII. Path-Goal Theory: Emphasizes a leader's role in removing obstacles to help employees achieve their goals.

XIV. Situational Leadership: Suggests that leaders must adjust their style based on the team's development, ranging from directive to supportive.

XV. Autocratic Leadership: A style where leaders make decisions unilaterally, expecting compliance without input from the team.

XVI. Democratic Leadership: A style that involves team members in decision-making, fostering collaboration and boosting morale.

XVII. Laissez-faire Leadership: A hands-off approach where leaders give autonomy to skilled teams, though it can result in a lack of direction if poorly managed.

XVIII. Transactional Leadership: A leadership style based on rewards and punishments, with leaders setting clear goals and motivating performance through incentives.

XIX. Transformational Leadership: Leaders inspire followers by creating a compelling vision and encouraging employees to surpass their own expectations.

XX. Servant Leadership: Leaders prioritize the needs, growth, and well-being of their team members, believing that serving their team leads to better results.

XXI. Authentic Leadership: A leadership style characterized by genuine, transparent actions, fostering trust and loyalty through consistency, integrity, and ethics.

XXII. Corporate Governance: The system by which companies are directed and controlled, focusing on ethical leadership, corporate culture, and decision-making.

XXIII. Ethical Leadership: Leaders who emphasize integrity, transparency, and ethical decision-making, setting the tone for corporate values and behaviors.

XXIV. Corporate Culture: The shared values, beliefs, and norms within an organization, heavily influenced by leadership.

XXV. Leadership Development Frameworks: Models for developing leadership skills, such as the 70-20-10 model, which attributes 70% of learning to on-the-job experiences, 20% to feedback and interactions, and 10% to formal education.

XXVI. Emotional Intelligence (EQ): The ability of leaders to understand and manage their own emotions and those of others, promoting empathy and effective leadership.

XXVII. Conflict Management: The ability to mediate and resolve conflicts constructively, creating a positive work environment.

XXVIII. Delegation and Empowerment: Leaders distribute tasks and grant autonomy to employees, building trust and enhancing team performance.

XXIX. Decision-Making: A crucial leadership skill that involves making informed and timely decisions while considering team input.

XXX. Global Leadership: Leadership within multinational organizations, requiring cultural sensitivity, adaptability, and cross-cultural management skills.

XXXI. Strategic Leadership: Focuses on creating and implementing long-term goals that align with the organization's vision, requiring vision articulation and effective resource management.

XXXII. John Kotter's 8-Step Change Model: A framework for leading organizations through change, emphasizing urgency, guiding coalitions, and anchoring new approaches into culture.

XXXIII. Succession Planning: The process of identifying and developing future leaders to ensure the organization's long-term success and continuity.

XXXIV. Performance Appraisal Systems: Tools used by HR to assess leadership potential, helping to identify areas for growth and improvement.

XXXV. Employee Engagement Surveys: Tools used to measure how engaged employees are, often reflecting the quality of leadership.

XXXVI. 360-Degree Feedback: A comprehensive feedback system where leaders receive input from peers, subordinates, and supervisors to assess their leadership effectiveness.

XXXVII. Crisis Management: The ability of leaders to guide their organization through crises, maintaining calm, decisiveness, and compassion.

XXXVIII. Innovation Leadership: Leadership that encourages a culture of innovation, empowering employees to contribute new ideas and take creative risks.

XXXIX. High-Performance Culture: An organizational culture driven by strong leadership that emphasizes accountability, innovation, and collaboration.

Chapter 5: Data-Driven HR Strategy

Part 1: Introduction to Data-Driven HR

The landscape of Human Resources (HR) has evolved dramatically over the past few decades. Traditionally, HR was seen primarily as an administrative function responsible for managing employee records, payroll, and compliance with labor laws. However, as businesses have become more complex and competitive, the role of HR has expanded to encompass strategic elements such as talent acquisition, employee engagement, and organizational development. This transformation has been driven, in large part, by the integration of data and analytics into HR practices, giving rise to what is now known as data-driven HR.

Data-driven HR systematically uses data and analytics to inform HR decisions, strategies, and processes. It involves collecting, analyzing, and interpreting data from various sources, including employee performance metrics, recruitment statistics, and employee engagement surveys. The goal is to leverage this data to make more informed and objective decisions that align with the organization's overall business strategy.

1.1 The Shift from Traditional to Data-Driven HR

In the past, HR decisions were often based on intuition, experience, or anecdotal evidence. While these approaches have their merits, they can also lead to inconsistencies and biases that hinder the effectiveness of HR initiatives. Data-driven HR, on the other hand, offers a more objective and evidence-based approach to decision-making. By analyzing large volumes of data, HR professionals can identify patterns, predict outcomes, and develop strategies grounded in empirical evidence.

For example, consider the traditional approach to employee recruitment. HR managers might rely on gut feeling or the subjective opinions of interviewers to make hiring decisions. In a data-driven HR framework, these decisions would be supplemented with data-driven insights, such as predictive analytics that assess a candidate's likelihood of success in the role based on historical data. This improves the quality of hires and reduces the time and cost associated with the recruitment process.

1.2 The Importance of Data in Modern HR Practices

The increasing availability of data and advanced analytics tools has revolutionized how organizations approach HR management. Data-driven HR enables organizations to:

1. Enhance Decision-Making: By providing objective insights, data-driven HR reduces reliance on guesswork and helps HR professionals make better-informed decisions. Whether it's determining the best candidates to hire, identifying employees at risk of leaving or designing effective training programs, data-driven decisions are more likely to achieve desired outcomes.
2. Increase Efficiency: Data analytics can streamline HR processes, reducing the time and effort required to complete tasks. For instance, automated resume screening tools can quickly identify qualified candidates, freeing up HR staff to focus on more strategic activities. Similarly, data-driven performance management systems can automate the collection and analysis of employee

performance data, making it easier to identify top performers and those who may need additional support.
3. Improve Employee Experience: Understanding employee sentiment and engagement levels through data can lead to more targeted and effective interventions. For example, pulse surveys can provide real-time feedback on employee morale, allowing HR to address issues before they escalate. Data-driven HR can also personalize employee experiences, offering customized career development plans or wellness programs based on individual needs and preferences.
4. Align HR with Business Objectives: Data-driven HR ensures that HR strategies align closely with the organization's overall goals. By analyzing data on workforce trends, HR can anticipate future challenges and opportunities, such as skills shortages or changes in employee demographics. This proactive approach enables organizations to stay competitive in a rapidly changing business environment.

1.3. The Growing Role of Big Data and Analytics in HR

The advent of big data and advanced analytics has further amplified the impact of data-driven HR. Big data refers to the vast amounts of structured and unstructured data generated by digital interactions, social media, sensors, and other sources. In HR, big data can include everything from employee demographics and work history to social media activity and feedback from exit interviews.

Advanced analytics techniques, such as machine learning and predictive modeling, can process this data to uncover hidden patterns and correlations that would be impossible to detect manually. For example, predictive analytics can forecast employee turnover by analyzing job satisfaction, workload, and external job market conditions. Machine learning algorithms can improve over time, continually refining their predictions as more data becomes available.

By harnessing the power of big data and analytics, data-driven HR allows organizations to move from reactive to proactive workforce management. Instead of simply responding to problems as they arise, HR can anticipate challenges and take preemptive action to mitigate risks and capitalize on opportunities.

1.4. The Strategic Impact of Data-Driven HR

As organizations continue to navigate an increasingly complex and competitive global landscape, the strategic importance of data-driven HR cannot be overstated. Organizations can achieve various benefits by aligning HR practices with data-driven insights, from improved employee retention and engagement to enhanced organizational agility and innovation.

However, the transition to a data-driven HR approach has challenges. HR professionals must develop the necessary skills to interpret and apply data insights effectively. Additionally, organizations must invest in the right technologies and infrastructure to support data collection, storage, and analysis. Ethical considerations, such as data privacy and the potential for algorithmic bias, must also be carefully managed.

In conclusion, data-driven HR represents a paradigm shift in how organizations manage their workforce. By embracing data and analytics, HR can move beyond its traditional administrative role to become a key driver of business success. As we explore the various components and applications of data-driven HR in this textbook, it will become clear that this approach is not just a trend but a fundamental change in how HR contributes to organizational performance.

Part 2: The Evolution of HR: From Administrative to Strategic

Human Resources (HR) has undergone a significant transformation over the past century, evolving from a purely administrative function into a key strategic partner within organizations. This evolution reflects broader changes in the business environment, including globalization, technological advancements, and the growing recognition of people as a critical asset to organizational success. Understanding this evolution provides context for the emergence of data-driven HR, representing the latest stage in this ongoing transformation.

2.1. The Early Days: HR as an Administrative Function

In its earliest incarnation, the HR function was primarily concerned with administrative tasks related to managing a workforce. In the late 19th and early 20th centuries, during the Industrial Revolution, organizations began to formalize their labor management, giving rise to what was then known as "personnel management." This role was largely reactive, focused on tasks such as record-keeping, payroll processing, and ensuring compliance with labor laws and regulations.

Personnel managers were responsible for hiring and firing workers, managing employee benefits, and handling disputes between employees and employers. The focus was on maintaining order and ensuring the workforce complies with company policies and government regulations. This role was essential but often viewed as a support function, separate from the core activities that drove business success.

2.2. The Shift to Human Resources: Recognizing the Value of People

The mid-20th century began a shift in how organizations viewed their workforce. As businesses grew in size and complexity, the limitations of a purely administrative approach to workforce management became apparent. The emergence of management and organizational behavior theories, such as those proposed by Elton Mayo and Abraham Maslow, highlighted the importance of employee motivation, engagement, and well-being. These theories suggested that treating employees as valuable resources rather than just inputs to production could lead to better performance and organizational outcomes.

This shift in perspective led to the rebranding of "personnel management" as "human resources," reflecting a broader and more strategic understanding of the role. HR departments began to focus on administrative tasks and initiatives to develop and retain talent, improve employee satisfaction, and align workforce capabilities with organizational goals.

During this period, HR professionals took on new responsibilities, including recruitment and selection, training and development, performance management, and organizational development. The role of HR began to expand beyond the confines of administrative tasks as HR professionals were increasingly involved in shaping workplace culture, developing leadership capabilities, and implementing policies that promoted employee well-being and productivity.

2.3. The Strategic Era: HR as a Business Partner

The 1980s and 1990s witnessed a further evolution in the role of HR, driven by changes in the global business environment. As competition intensified and technological change accelerated, organizations recognized that their ability to attract, develop, and retain top talent was a key determinant of success. This realization led to "strategic HR," where HR was seen as a support function and a vital contributor to the organization's strategy and competitive advantage.

Strategic HR emphasizes the alignment of HR practices with the overall business strategy. In this era, HR professionals must understand the business's objectives and challenges and design HR strategies to support achieving these goals. This involves a deep understanding of workforce dynamics, labor markets, and the external environment and the ability to anticipate future needs and trends.

2.4. Key aspects of strategic HR include:

Talent Management: Developing comprehensive strategies for attracting, developing, and retaining the best talent. This includes succession planning, leadership development, and fostering a strong organizational culture.

Workforce Planning: Analyzing current and future workforce needs ensures the organization has the right people with the right skills and roles at the right time.

Performance Management: Creating systems that align employee performance with organizational goals, including setting clear expectations, providing regular feedback, and linking rewards to performance.

Change Management: Leading organizational change initiatives, such as mergers, acquisitions, or digital transformation, and ensuring employees are engaged and supported throughout the process.

Employee Engagement and Well-being: Developing strategies to enhance employee satisfaction, motivation, and overall well-being, recognizing that a motivated and healthy workforce is essential for sustained success.

2.5. The Emergence of Data-Driven HR: A New Frontier

The 21st century has ushered in a new era for HR, driven by the rise of big data, analytics, and advanced technologies. The strategic role of HR has been further enhanced by the ability to leverage data to make more informed decisions, predict trends, and measure the impact of HR initiatives on business outcomes. This data-driven approach allows HR to move from being a reactive function to a proactive one, anticipating challenges and opportunities and positioning the organization for long-term success.

Data-driven HR represents the convergence of traditional HR practices with modern data science and technology. It involves collecting and analyzing data from various sources, such as employee surveys, performance metrics, and external labor market data, to inform HR strategies and decision-making.

Predictive analytics, machine learning, and artificial intelligence in HR have transformed how organizations manage their workforce, enabling more precise and effective interventions in areas such as recruitment, retention, and employee development.

Conclusion: The Strategic Importance of HR

The evolution of HR from an administrative to a strategic function reflects the growing recognition of people's critical role in organizational success. As businesses face increasingly complex challenges in a rapidly changing environment, the ability to manage and develop talent has become a key source of competitive advantage. The emergence of data-driven HR is the latest step in this evolution. It offers new tools and insights that enable HR professionals to contribute more effectively to their organization's strategic goals.

Today, HR is not just a function that manages people; it is a strategic partner that drives business success by aligning human capital with organizational objectives. As we continue to explore the components and applications of data-driven HR in this textbook, it will become clear that integrating data and analytics into HR practices is not just an enhancement but a fundamental shift in how HR contributes to the overall performance and sustainability of organizations.

Part 3: Defining Data-Driven HR

In the rapidly evolving human resources (HR) landscape, data-driven HR has emerged as a transformative approach that redefines how organizations manage their most valuable asset—people. At its core, data-driven HR leverages data, analytics, and technology to inform, optimize, and innovate HR practices. This approach moves HR from a reactive, intuition-based function to a proactive, evidence-based strategic partner, fundamentally altering how decisions and actions are taken within the HR domain.

3.1. Understanding Data-Driven HR

Data-driven HR systematically uses data and analytics to enhance and inform HR decision-making processes. It encompasses collecting, analyzing, and interpreting data related to various HR functions—such as recruitment, performance management, employee engagement, learning and development, and workforce planning—to drive more effective and efficient outcomes.

The concept of data-driven HR is built on the premise that better access to data, coupled with advanced analytical tools, can significantly improve the accuracy and impact of HR decisions. Instead of relying solely on experience, intuition, or industry best practices, HR professionals can now make decisions based on empirical evidence tailored to their organization's needs.

3.2. The Importance of Data in Modern HR Practices

✓ The transition to data-driven HR is not merely a trend; it is a fundamental shift that offers numerous benefits to organizations:

- ✓ **Enhanced Accuracy and Objectivity:** Data-driven HR minimizes the influence of biases and subjective judgments in decision-making. By relying on factual data, organizations can make more accurate and objective decisions, leading to better outcomes for the business and its employees.

- ✓ **Strategic Alignment:** Data-driven HR ensures that HR strategies align closely with the organization's overall business objectives. For example, by analyzing workforce data, HR can identify critical skills gaps that must be addressed to support the company's strategic goals.

- ✓ **Increased Efficiency:** Data and analytics can streamline HR processes, reducing the time and resources required to perform various HR tasks. For example, automated data analysis tools can quickly identify trends or issues, allowing HR professionals to focus on more strategic activities.

- ✓ **Proactive Management:** With predictive and prescriptive analytics, HR can anticipate future challenges and opportunities rather than simply reacting to them. For instance, predictive models can identify employees at risk of leaving, allowing HR to implement retention strategies before turnover becomes problematic.

- ✓ **Improved Employee Experience:** By leveraging data to understand employee needs and preferences, HR can create more personalized and engaging employee experiences. For example, data-driven insights can inform the design of tailored career development programs or wellness initiatives that resonate with employees.

3.3. Applications of Data-Driven HR

Data-driven HR can be applied across a wide range of HR functions, including:

i. **Talent Acquisition:** Analyzing recruitment data to identify the most effective sourcing channels, predict candidate success, and reduce time-to-hire.

ii. **Performance Management:** Using data to set realistic performance goals, track progress, and provide targeted feedback.

iii. **Employee Retention:** Identifying factors that contribute to employee turnover and developing data-informed strategies to improve retention.

iv. **Learning and Development:** Assessing skills gaps and designing training programs that address the workforce's specific needs.

v. **Diversity, Equity, and Inclusion (DEI):** Measuring diversity metrics, identifying biases in HR processes, and developing data-driven DEI initiatives.

3.4. Challenges in Implementing Data-Driven HR

While the benefits of data-driven HR are clear, implementing this approach is not without challenges:

- ➢ **Data Quality and Availability:** Ensuring that the data collected is accurate, complete, and relevant is essential for reliable analysis. Poor data quality can lead to incorrect conclusions and ineffective decisions.

- Technology and Tools: Implementing the necessary technology and tools to collect, store, and analyze data can be complex and costly. Organizations must invest in the right platforms and ensure that HR professionals are trained to use them effectively.
- Privacy and Ethical Concerns: Using employee data raises important privacy and ethical considerations. Organizations must be transparent about how data is collected and used, and ensure that they comply with relevant regulations and ethical standards.
- Change Management: Transitioning to a data-driven approach requires a cultural shift within the HR team and the broader organization. HR professionals must embrace data-driven decision-making and develop the necessary skills to analyze and interpret data.

3.5. Foundational Concepts in Data-Driven HR

In today's rapidly evolving business environment, the role of Human Resources (HR) has expanded beyond traditional functions to include a strategic focus on data-driven decision-making. Data-Driven HR refers to the practice of leveraging data, analytics, and evidence-based approaches to improve HR practices, enhance organizational performance, and drive business outcomes. This chapter introduces the foundational concepts that underpin Data-Driven HR, providing a framework for understanding how data can be utilized effectively within HR functions.

3.5.5. Data in HR serves several key purposes:

Improving Decision-Making: By analyzing employee data, HR professionals can make more informed decisions about recruitment, retention, training, and development.

Enhancing Employee Experience: Data can be used to identify trends and patterns in employee behavior, enabling HR to create a more personalized and engaging employee experience.

Driving Business Outcomes: Data-driven HR practices contribute to achieving business goals by optimizing workforce performance and aligning HR strategies with overall business strategy.

3.6. Key Components of Data-Driven HR

Data Collection

The foundation of Data-Driven HR is the collection of accurate and relevant data. This includes data on employee demographics, performance metrics, engagement surveys, and more. Effective data collection involves selecting the right tools and technologies to gather data consistently and ethically.

Data Analysis

Once data is collected, the next step is analysis. This involves applying statistical techniques to interpret the data and uncover insights. Common methods include descriptive analytics (summarizing data), predictive analytics (forecasting future trends), and prescriptive analytics (recommending actions based on data).

Data Interpretation and Action

The insights gained from data analysis must be interpreted within the organization's goals and objectives. HR professionals must translate data findings into actionable strategies addressing specific HR challenges and opportunities. This step is crucial for ensuring that data-driven decisions lead to tangible improvements in HR practices and business outcomes.

3.7. The Role of Technology in Data-Driven HR

Technology plays a critical role in enabling Data-Driven HR. Tools such as Human Resource Information Systems (HRIS), Applicant Tracking Systems (ATS), and HR analytics platforms provide the infrastructure needed to collect, store, and analyze HR data. Additionally, advancements in artificial intelligence (AI) and machine learning are opening new possibilities for predictive and prescriptive analytics in HR.

3.8. Ethical Considerations in Data-Driven HR

As HR becomes increasingly data-driven, it is essential to consider the ethical implications of using employee data. This section explores key ethical considerations, including data privacy, consent, and transparency. HR professionals must balance the benefits of data-driven practices with the responsibility to protect employees' rights and maintain trust.

3.9. Challenges in Implementing Data-Driven HR

- ✓ **Data Quality:** Ensuring the accuracy and reliability of HR data.
- ✓ **Skill Gaps:** Developing the necessary analytical skills within the HR team.
- ✓ **Resistance to Change:** Overcoming organizational culture that may be resistant to adopting data-driven practices.
- ✓ **Integration of Systems:** Ensuring that different HR systems and data sources are compatible.

Part 4: The Future of Data-Driven HR

Data-Driven HR is rapidly evolving, with new trends and technologies emerging. The future of HR will likely see greater integration of AI, more sophisticated analytics capabilities, and a continued emphasis on aligning HR practices with business strategy through data. This section explores potential future developments and their implications for HR professionals.

Data-Driven HR represents a significant shift in how HR functions within organizations. By leveraging data, HR can move from being a transactional support function to a strategic partner that drives business outcomes. Understanding the foundational concepts of Data-Driven HR is the first step toward building a more effective and impactful HR practice.

4.1. Types of HR Data: Quantitative vs. Qualitative

In Data-Driven HR, understanding the available data types is crucial for effective decision-making. HR data can be broadly categorized into two main types: quantitative and qualitative. Each data type provides unique insights into the workforce, and understanding their differences, strengths, and limitations is essential for HR professionals. This chapter delves into the characteristics of quantitative and qualitative HR data, exploring how each can be utilized to inform HR practices and strategies.

Quantitative HR data refers to data that can be measured and expressed numerically. It is typically structured, making it easier to analyze and compare. This data type is often derived from HR information systems, surveys, and other tools that capture employee metrics in a standardized format.

4.2. Key characteristics of quantitative HR data include:

- Numerical Representation: Data is expressed in numbers, allowing for statistical analysis.
- Objectivity: Quantitative data is less prone to subjective interpretation.
- Measurability: This data type can be measured, compared, and tracked over time.

Quantitative data in HR is collected from various sources, including:

- Employee Demographics: Age, gender, education level, years of service.
- Performance Metrics: Sales figures, productivity levels, customer satisfaction scores.
- Engagement Surveys: Numerical responses to standardized survey questions.
- Compensation Data: Salary, bonuses, benefits.

Numerical Representation	**Data is expressed in numbers, allowing for statistical analysis.**
Objectivity	Quantitative data is less prone to subjective interpretation.
Measurability	This data type can be measured, compared, and tracked over time.
Quantitative data in HR is collected from various sources, including:	
Employee Demographics	Age, gender, education level, years of service.
Performance Metrics	Sales figures, productivity levels, customer satisfaction scores.
Engagement Surveys	Numerical responses to standardized survey questions.
Compensation Data	Salary, bonuses, benefits.

Part 5: Advantages of Quantitative HR Data

Quantitative data offers several advantages:

Ease of Analysis: Due to its numerical nature, quantitative data can be analyzed using statistical methods, making it easier to identify trends and patterns.

Comparability: Data can be compared across different groups, time periods, and benchmarks, providing insights into performance and areas for improvement.

Scalability: Quantitative data can be scaled across large organizations, providing a broad view of HR-related outcomes.

5.1. Limitations of Quantitative HR Data

Despite its strengths, quantitative data has limitations:

a) Lack of Context: Numbers alone may not provide the full picture, missing the underlying reasons behind the data.

b) Rigidity: Standardized data collection methods may not capture the complexity of human behavior and experiences.

c) Over-reliance on Numbers: Focusing solely on quantitative data can lead to ignoring qualitative insights that are crucial for understanding the workforce.

Part 6: Qualitative HR Data

Qualitative HR data, in contrast, is non-numerical and descriptive in nature. It captures the complexity of human experiences, emotions, and behaviors, providing deeper insights into employee attitudes, motivations, and perceptions. Qualitative data is often gathered through interviews, focus groups, open-ended survey questions, and observations.

Key characteristics of qualitative HR data include:

- ✓ Descriptive Nature: Data is expressed in words, providing rich, detailed insights.
- ✓ Subjectivity: Qualitative data is often interpretive and may vary based on the perspective of the data collector or respondent.
- ✓ Contextual Depth: This data type provides context and understanding of the 'why' behind employee behaviors and outcomes.

6.1. Common Sources of Qualitative HR Data

Qualitative data in HR is typically gathered from:

- ➤ Interviews: In-depth discussions with employees or focus groups that explore their experiences, opinions, and feelings.

- ➢ Observations: Behavioral observations in the workplace, capturing how employees interact and respond in different situations.
- ➢ Open-Ended Survey Responses: Responses that allow employees to express their thoughts and feelings in their own words.

Employee Feedback: Comments and suggestions from employees through various channels, such as suggestion boxes or internal communication platforms.

6.2. Advantages of Qualitative HR Data

Qualitative data offers several unique advantages:

Richness of Information: Provides detailed insights into employee experiences and the reasons behind their actions.

Flexibility: Can adapt to capture complex and evolving human behaviors and emotions.

Understanding Context: Helps HR professionals understand the context of quantitative findings, providing a more holistic view of workforce issues.

6.3. Limitations of Qualitative HR Data

However, qualitative data also has its limitations:

Subjectivity: Data can be influenced by personal biases and interpretations, leading to inconsistencies.

Time-Consuming: Collecting and analyzing qualitative data is often more time-consuming and resource-intensive than quantitative data.

Challenges in Analysis: Analyzing qualitative data requires specialized skills, and the results are not easily generalizable.

6.4. Advantages of Qualitative HR Data

Richness of Information: Provides detailed insights into employee experiences and the reasons behind their actions.

Flexibility: Can adapt to capture complex and evolving human behaviors and emotions.

Understanding Context: Helps HR professionals understand the context of quantitative findings, providing a more holistic view of workforce issues.

6.5. Limitations of Qualitative HR Data

Subjectivity: Data can be influenced by personal biases and interpretations, leading to inconsistencies.

Time-Consuming: Collecting and analyzing qualitative data is often more time-consuming and resource-intensive than quantitative data.

Challenges in Analysis: Analyzing qualitative data requires specialized skills, and the results are not easily generalizable.

Part 7: Integrating Quantitative and Qualitative Data

The Complementary Nature of Quantitative and Qualitative Data

While quantitative and qualitative data have distinct characteristics, they are most powerful when used together. Integrating both types of data allows HR professionals to understand workforce dynamics comprehensively. Quantitative data can highlight trends and patterns, while qualitative data can explain the reasons behind those patterns.

Practical Examples of Data Integration

Employee Engagement: Quantitative data from engagement surveys can show overall satisfaction levels, while qualitative data from interviews can reveal areas where employees feel disengaged.

Performance Management: Quantitative performance metrics can identify high and low performers, while qualitative feedback can provide insights into the behaviors and attitudes contributing to those performance levels.

Turnover Analysis: Quantitative data can track turnover rates, while qualitative exit interviews can uncover why employees leave.

7.1. Challenges in Using HR Data

Ensuring Data Quality

Whether working with quantitative or qualitative data, ensuring data quality is crucial. This includes accuracy, reliability, and validity of the data collected. Poor data quality can lead to incorrect conclusions and misguided HR strategies.

Balancing Data Types

HR professionals must balance quantitative and qualitative data to avoid over-reliance on one type. This balance ensures that decisions are well-rounded and informed by numbers and narratives.

Overcoming Data Silos

Data silos can prevent the effective integration of quantitative and qualitative data. Organizations must ensure that data is accessible across departments and that there is a culture of collaboration in data analysis.

Conclusion

Understanding the types of HR data—quantitative and qualitative—is foundational for Data-Driven HR. Each type of data has its own strengths and limitations, and when used together, they provide a richer, more nuanced understanding of the workforce. By integrating quantitative and qualitative data, HR professionals can make more informed, evidence-based decisions that enhance organizational performance and employee well-being.

7.2. Key Metrics and KPIs in HR

In Human Resources (HR), metrics and Key Performance Indicators (KPIs) are essential tools for measuring the effectiveness and impact of HR practices. These metrics provide quantifiable data that can be used to assess the performance of various HR functions, guide strategic decision-making, and demonstrate the value of HR to the broader organization. This chapter explores the key metrics and KPIs in HR, their importance, and how they can be utilized to drive organizational success.

Understanding HR Metrics and KPIs

7.2.1 Definition of HR Metrics

HR metrics are specific, quantifiable measures that track HR processes' efficiency, effectiveness, and impact. These metrics provide data on various HR activities, from recruitment and onboarding to employee engagement and turnover.

7.3. Key characteristics of HR metrics include:

Quantifiability: Metrics are numerical and allow for easy comparison over time.

Specificity: They focus on specific aspects of HR functions, providing targeted insights.

Actionability: Metrics are used to inform decisions and guide improvements in HR practices.

7.4. Definition of KPIs in HR

Key Performance Indicators (KPIs) are a subset of HR metrics that are directly linked to the organization's strategic goals. KPIs are the critical indicators of progress toward achieving specific business objectives. While all KPIs are metrics, not all metrics qualify as KPIs.

7.5. Key characteristics of KPIs include:

Strategic Alignment: KPIs are aligned with the organization's overall strategy and objectives.

Outcome-Focused: They focus on the results and outcomes that matter most to the business.

Measurable Targets: KPIs often have specific targets or benchmarks that define success.

7.6. The Role of Metrics and KPIs in HR

Metrics and KPIs play a crucial role in HR by:

Measuring Performance: They provide a way to evaluate the effectiveness of HR initiatives and processes.

Driving Decision-Making: Data from metrics and KPIs help HR professionals make informed decisions that align with business objectives.

Demonstrating Value: By quantifying the impact of HR activities, metrics and KPIs help demonstrate the value of HR to organizational leaders.

7.7. Key HR Metrics and KPIs

Recruitment Metrics

Time to Fill: The average number of days it takes to fill an open position. This metric helps assess the efficiency of the recruitment process.

Cost per Hire: The total cost of recruiting a new employee, including advertising, agency fees, and other related expenses. This KPI is critical for budgeting and optimizing recruitment spending.

Quality of Hire: A measure of how well new hires perform compared to expectations. It can be assessed through performance reviews, retention rates, or productivity levels.

Offer Acceptance Rate: The percentage of job offers that candidates accept. A low rate may indicate issues with the compensation package or recruitment process.

Employee Engagement Metrics

Employee Satisfaction Score: A measure of employees' satisfaction with their jobs, typically assessed through surveys. High satisfaction levels are linked to better performance and lower turnover.

Employee Net Promoter Score (eNPS): A metric that gauges employee loyalty and their likelihood to recommend the organization as a great workplace.

Absenteeism Rate: The average number of days employees are absent from work. High absenteeism can indicate low engagement or potential issues in the workplace.

Turnover Rate: The percentage of employees who leave the organization during a specific period. This KPI is crucial for understanding retention issues and the workforce's overall health.

Performance and Productivity Metrics

Revenue per Employee: The total revenue generated by the organization divided by the number of employees. This KPI measures the productivity and effectiveness of the workforce.

Performance Appraisal Scores: Average scores from employee performance reviews provide insights into overall employee performance levels.

Training ROI: The return on investment (ROI) for training programs, calculated by comparing the cost of training to the benefits gained, such as increased productivity or reduced errors.

Goal Completion Rate: The percentage of employee or team goals that are achieved within a given timeframe, reflecting the effectiveness of performance management practices.

7.8. Compensation and Benefits Metrics

Compensation Ratio: The ratio of an employee's salary to the midpoint of the salary range for their position. This metric helps ensure fair and competitive compensation practices.

Benefits Participation Rate: The percentage of employees who participate in optional benefits programs, indicating the attractiveness and relevance of offered benefits.

Overtime Rate: The percentage of total hours worked that are overtime. High overtime rates can indicate workload issues or staffing shortages.

Pay Equity: The ratio of pay between different groups of employees, often used to assess and address potential pay disparities.

Health and Safety Metrics

Workplace Injury Rate: The number of workplace injuries per 100 full-time employees during a given period. This metric is critical for assessing workplace safety.

Lost Time Injury Frequency Rate (LTIFR): The number of lost time injuries per million hours worked. This KPI is used to monitor and improve workplace safety programs.

Health and Wellness Program Participation: The percentage of employees participating in health and wellness programs, reflecting the effectiveness of these initiatives in promoting employee well-being.

Employee Assistance Program (EAP) Utilization Rate: The percentage of employees using EAP services, which can indicate the level of stress or personal issues in the workforce.

7.9. Developing and Implementing HR Metrics and KPIs

Identifying Relevant Metrics and KPIs

When developing HR metrics and KPIs, it is essential to align them with the organization's strategic objectives. HR professionals should:

Understand Business Goals: Identify the key business objectives that HR can influence, such as reducing turnover, improving employee engagement, or enhancing productivity.

Select Relevant Metrics: Choose metrics that directly relate to these goals and provide actionable insights.

Set Measurable Targets: Establish clear, measurable targets for each KPI, ensuring they are realistic and aligned with business priorities.

7.10. Data Collection and Analysis

Effective data collection and analysis are crucial for tracking HR metrics and KPIs:

Data Sources: Utilize various data sources, including HRIS, surveys, and performance management systems, to gather the necessary data.

Data Accuracy: Ensure the data collected is accurate, consistent, and up-to-date, as poor data quality can lead to misleading conclusions.

Regular Monitoring: Continuously monitor metrics and KPIs, and analyze trends over time to identify areas for improvement.

7.11. Communicating Metrics and KPIs

Clear communication of HR metrics and KPIs is vital for their effectiveness:

Reporting: Develop regular reports that highlight key metrics and KPIs, using visual aids such as charts and graphs to make the data more accessible.

Stakeholder Engagement: Share insights with relevant stakeholders, including senior management, to demonstrate the impact of HR initiatives and guide strategic decisions.

Continuous Improvement: Use the feedback from stakeholders to refine metrics, improve data collection methods, and adjust HR strategies as needed.

7.12. Challenges in Using HR Metrics and KPIs

Data Integration and Consistency

One of the main challenges in using HR metrics and KPIs is ensuring data integration and consistency across different systems and departments. Disparate data sources can lead to inconsistencies, making obtaining a comprehensive view of HR performance difficult.

Over-Reliance on Metrics

While metrics and KPIs are valuable tools, over-reliance on them can lead to a narrow focus on quantitative data at the expense of qualitative insights. HR professionals should balance metrics with an understanding of the broader context.

Aligning KPIs with Changing Business Goals

As business goals evolve, so do the HR metrics and KPIs. Ensuring these metrics remain aligned with the organization's priorities can be challenging, requiring continuous review and adjustment.

7.13. The Future of HR Metrics and KPIs

The future of HR metrics and KPIs is likely to be shaped by technological advances, particularly in big data, machine learning, and predictive analytics. These technologies will enable more sophisticated analysis and forecasting, allowing HR professionals to anticipate trends and make more proactive decisions.

Moreover, as organizations increasingly recognize the strategic value of HR, there will be a growing emphasis on developing metrics that not only measure HR's impact but also contribute to broader business success. This shift will require HR professionals to enhance their data analytics capabilities continuously and to remain agile in adapting to changing business environments.

Conclusion

HR metrics and KPIs are indispensable tools for measuring the effectiveness of HR practices and their impact on organizational performance. By understanding the key metrics and KPIs, HR professionals can make data-driven decisions that align with business objectives and demonstrate the value of HR to the organization. As the role of HR continues to evolve, the ability to effectively use metrics and KPIs will be crucial for driving strategic success.

Part 8: The Role of Big Data in HR Management

In the modern business landscape, the proliferation of data has transformed various organizational functions, including Human Resources (HR). Big Data, characterized by its volume, velocity, and variety, has emerged as a powerful tool in HR management. By leveraging Big Data, HR professionals can gain deeper insights into workforce trends, improve decision-making processes, and enhance the overall effectiveness of HR practices. This chapter explores the role of Big Data in HR management, its applications, benefits, challenges, and the future potential it holds for the HR field.

8.1. Understanding Big Data in HR

Definition of Big Data

Big Data refers to extensive and complex data sets that traditional data processing software cannot manage effectively. These data sets are generated from various sources, including social media, employee interactions, sensors, and transactional systems. In HR, Big Data encompasses all the information related to employees, candidates, and workforce processes.

8.2. Key characteristics of Big Data include:

Volume: The sheer amount of data generated by various HR activities and external sources.

Velocity: The speed at which new data is created and needs to be processed.

Variety: The diverse types of data, including structured, unstructured, and semi-structured data.

8.3. The Relevance of Big Data to HR

Big Data is increasingly relevant to HR because it enables more informed decision-making. By analyzing large volumes of data, HR professionals can uncover patterns and trends that would be impossible to detect with traditional data analysis methods. This shift towards data-driven HR management has the potential to revolutionize how organizations attract, retain, and develop talent.

8.4. Applications of Big Data in HR

Talent Acquisition and Recruitment

Predictive Analytics in Hiring: Big Data allows HR professionals to predict which candidates are most likely to succeed in specific roles by analyzing historical data on successful hires, candidate characteristics, and interview outcomes. Predictive models can identify key predictors of job performance, reducing the risk of bad hires.

Social Media and Recruitment: Analyzing social media data provides insights into candidates' personalities, interests, and professional networks. This information can complement traditional recruitment methods, helping HR teams to identify potential talent earlier and more effectively.

Candidate Experience Optimization: Big Data can be used to analyze candidate feedback and behavior during the recruitment process, enabling HR to continuously improve the candidate experience, reduce drop-off rates, and enhance employer branding.

Employee Engagement and Retention

Sentiment Analysis: By analyzing employee feedback, emails, and social media activity, HR can gauge overall employee sentiment and identify potential areas of dissatisfaction. This proactive approach allows organizations to address issues before they lead to turnover.

Turnover Prediction: Big Data enables HR to identify patterns and risk factors associated with employee turnover. Predictive models can be developed to forecast which employees are most likely to leave, allowing for timely interventions to improve retention.

Personalized Engagement Strategies: With Big Data, HR can tailor engagement strategies to different employee segments based on their behavior, preferences, and performance. This personalized approach enhances employee satisfaction and productivity.

Performance Management and Development

Real-Time Performance Monitoring: Big Data allows for continuous, real-time monitoring of employee performance through various data sources, including project management tools, customer feedback, and sales data. This real-time feedback helps managers to make more timely and informed decisions.

Learning and Development Analytics: By analyzing data from learning management systems (LMS), HR can identify the most effective training programs, tailor learning paths to individual needs, and measure the ROI of development initiatives.

Career Pathing and Succession Planning: Big Data enables HR to map out optimal career paths for employees based on their skills, experiences, and aspirations. Predictive analytics can also help in identifying potential leaders and planning for succession, ensuring organizational continuity.

Workforce Planning and Analytics

Workforce Forecasting: Big Data helps HR forecast workforce needs by analyzing trends in business growth, market conditions, and employee demographics. This enables better planning for recruitment, training, and resource allocation.

Diversity and Inclusion Analysis: HR can monitor and improve diversity and inclusion efforts by analyzing demographic data. Big Data provides insights into the effectiveness of D&I initiatives, helping organizations to create a more inclusive workplace.

Compensation and Benefits Optimization: Big Data analytics can be used to assess the effectiveness of compensation and benefits programs. HR can analyze employee satisfaction, market trends, and financial performance data to optimize compensation strategies that attract and retain top talent.

8.5. Benefits of Big Data in HR Management

Enhanced Decision-Making

One of the primary benefits of Big Data in HR is the enhancement of decision-making processes. With access to vast amounts of data, HR professionals can make decisions based on evidence rather than intuition. This leads to more accurate and effective HR strategies that align with organizational goals.

Improved Talent Management

Big Data enables HR to better manage the entire employee lifecycle, from recruitment to retirement. By understanding the factors contributing to employee success and satisfaction, HR can implement targeted interventions to attract, develop, and retain talent.

Increased Efficiency and Productivity

By automating data collection and analysis, Big Data reduces the time and effort required for HR processes. This increased efficiency allows HR professionals to focus on strategic initiatives that drive organizational growth and productivity.

Enhanced Employee Experience

Big Data helps HR create a more satisfying and supportive work environment through personalized approaches to engagement, development, and career planning. This leads to higher employee morale, better performance, and reduced turnover.

8.6. Challenges of Big Data in HR

Data Privacy and Security

One of the significant challenges of Big Data in HR is ensuring data privacy and security. HR departments handle sensitive employee information; any breach can have severe legal and reputational consequences. Organizations must implement robust data protection measures to safeguard this information.

Data Integration and Quality

Big Data often comes from multiple sources, making data integration complex. Data quality and consistency is crucial, as inaccurate or incomplete data can lead to faulty conclusions and poor decision-making.

Skills Gap in HR Analytics

Effective use of Big Data in HR requires specialized data analysis, statistics, and technology skills. Many HR professionals may lack these skills, necessitating investment in training and development or hiring data science experts within the HR function.

Ethical Considerations

Using Big Data in HR raises ethical concerns, particularly around the potential for bias and discrimination in data-driven decisions. Organizations must ensure that their use of Big Data adheres to ethical standards and promotes fairness and transparency in HR practices.

8.7. The Future of Big Data in HR Management

Predictive and Prescriptive Analytics

As Big Data technology evolves, predictive and prescriptive analytics in HR will become more widespread. Predictive analytics will allow HR to anticipate future trends and challenges, while prescriptive analytics will provide actionable recommendations to optimize HR strategies.

Artificial Intelligence and Machine Learning

Integrating Artificial Intelligence (AI) and Machine Learning (ML) with Big Data will revolutionize HR management. These technologies will enable more sophisticated data analysis, automate routine tasks, and provide deeper insights into employee behavior and performance.

Real-Time HR Management

The future of Big Data in HR will shift towards real-time HR management. HR professionals can access and analyze data in real-time, allowing for immediate responses to emerging issues and opportunities. This will lead to more agile and responsive HR practices.

Data-Driven Culture in HR

As Big Data becomes integral to HR management, organizations will need to foster a data-driven culture within the HR function. This involves investing in technology and skills and encouraging a mindset that values data and evidence-based decision-making.

Conclusion

Big Data has the potential to transform HR management by providing deeper insights, enhancing decision-making, and improving the overall effectiveness of HR practices. While challenges are to be addressed, including data privacy, integration, and the need for new skills, the benefits of Big Data in HR are significant. As technology advances, the role of Big Data in HR will only grow, making it an essential tool for HR professionals in the 21st century.

Part 9. Applications of Data-Driven HR

The increasing availability of data and advances in analytics have revolutionized the Human Resources (HR) field. Data-driven HR refers to using data, metrics, and analytics to inform and enhance HR decision-making processes. By leveraging data, HR professionals can gain insights into employee behavior, optimize HR practices, and align HR strategies with organizational goals. This chapter explores the various applications of data-driven HR, illustrating how data can improve recruitment, employee engagement, performance management, workforce planning, and more.

Talent Acquisition and Recruitment Analytics

Predictive Hiring

Predictive hiring uses data analytics to forecast which candidates are most likely to succeed in a particular role. HR professionals can identify key attributes that predict success by analyzing historical data on previous hires, including their skills, experiences, and performance outcomes. This data-driven approach helps organizations make more informed hiring decisions, reducing the risk of poor hires and improving overall recruitment efficiency.

Candidate Sourcing Optimization

Data-driven HR can enhance candidate sourcing by analyzing data on where top candidates are found and which channels produce the highest quality applicants. By tracking metrics such as the source of hire, cost per hire, and time to fill, HR teams can optimize their sourcing strategies, focusing on the most effective channels and reducing recruitment costs.

Candidate Experience Enhancement

Improving the candidate experience is critical for attracting top talent. Data-driven HR allows organizations to analyze candidate feedback, application process data, and recruitment funnel metrics to identify pain points and areas for improvement. Organizations can continuously monitor and optimize the candidate experience to increase their offer acceptance rates and build a stronger employer brand.

Performance Management through Data

Continuous Performance Monitoring

Traditional performance management often relies on annual reviews, which can be subjective and untimely. Data-driven HR facilitates continuous performance monitoring by collecting real-time data on employee performance from various sources, such as project management tools, customer feedback, and peer evaluations. This ongoing feedback allows managers to provide timely guidance and support, fostering continuous improvement and development.

Talent Development and Succession Planning

Data-driven HR supports talent development and succession planning by identifying employees with high potential and tracking their progress over time. By analyzing data on skills, experiences, and performance, HR can create individualized development plans, prepare employees for future leadership roles, and ensure a robust talent pipeline for critical positions.

Employee Retention Strategies Informed by Data

Sentiment Analysis and Engagement Surveys

Employee engagement is a key driver of productivity and retention. Data-driven HR uses sentiment analysis and engagement surveys to assess employee morale and identify factors influencing engagement. By analyzing survey data, HR can identify trends, pinpoint areas of concern, and develop targeted initiatives to enhance employee engagement.

Predictive Retention Models

Predictive retention models use data to forecast which employees are at risk of leaving the organization. By analyzing factors such as job satisfaction, tenure, performance reviews, and external market conditions, HR can identify high-risk employees and take proactive steps to address their concerns. This data-driven approach helps reduce turnover and retain top talent.

Personalized Engagement Strategies

Data-driven HR enables the development of personalized engagement strategies tailored to individual employee needs and preferences. By analyzing data on employee behavior, preferences, and feedback, HR can design customized programs and initiatives that resonate with different employee segments, leading to higher satisfaction and retention rates.

Learning and Development Needs Assessment

Learning Needs Analysis

Data-driven HR supports learning and development (L&D) by identifying gaps in employee skills and knowledge. By analyzing performance data, employee feedback, and industry trends, HR can determine the learning needs of the workforce and design targeted training programs. This ensures that employees have the skills necessary to meet current and future organizational demands.

Measuring Training Effectiveness

Evaluating the effectiveness of training programs is essential for maximizing their impact. Data-driven HR enables the measurement of training effectiveness by analyzing metrics such as post-training performance, employee feedback, and ROI. This data-driven approach ensures that L&D initiatives are aligned with organizational goals and deliver tangible results.

Personalized Learning Pathways

Personalization is a key trend in L&D, and data-driven HR makes it possible to create customized learning pathways for employees. By analyzing data on individual learning preferences, career aspirations, and performance, HR can develop tailored training programs that support personal and professional growth, leading to higher employee engagement and development.

Compensation and Benefits Optimization

Compensation and benefits are critical components of employee satisfaction and retention. Data-driven HR allows organizations to analyze compensation data, benchmark against industry standards, and assess the impact of compensation strategies on employee retention and engagement. This analysis helps HR to design competitive compensation packages that attract and retain top talent while aligning with organizational budgets.

Part 10: Predictive Analytics in HR

Predictive analytics has emerged as a powerful tool in the field of Human Resources (HR), enabling organizations to anticipate future trends, identify potential risks, and make data-driven decisions that enhance workforce management. By analyzing historical data and applying statistical models, HR professionals can predict employee performance, retention, recruitment, and more outcomes. This chapter delves into the concept of predictive analytics in HR, exploring its applications, benefits, challenges, and the steps required to implement predictive analytics effectively within an organization.

Understanding Predictive Analytics in HR Context

Definition and Scope of Predictive Analytics

Predictive analytics involves using historical data, machine learning algorithms, and statistical techniques to forecast future events or behaviors. In HR, predictive analytics can be applied to a wide range of areas, including talent acquisition, employee retention, performance management, and workforce planning. Predictive analytics aims to provide actionable insights that help HR professionals make informed decisions that align with organizational goals.

10.1. The Predictive Analytics Process

The predictive analytics process typically involves the following steps:

Data Collection: Gathering relevant historical data from various sources, such as HR systems, employee surveys, performance reviews, and external market data.

Data Preparation: Cleaning and organizing the data to ensure accuracy and consistency. This may involve handling missing data, normalizing data formats, and selecting relevant variables for analysis.

Modeling: Selecting and applying statistical models or machine learning algorithms to the prepared data. Common techniques include regression analysis, decision trees, and neural networks.

Validation: Testing the predictive model on a subset of data to assess its accuracy and reliability. Adjustments may be made to improve the model's performance.

Deployment: Implementing the predictive model in HR processes to forecast outcomes and guide decision-making.

Monitoring and Refinement: Continuously monitor the model's performance and update it as new data becomes available or as organizational needs evolve.

10.2. Applications of Predictive Analytics in HR

Predicting Employee Turnover and Retention

Predictive Hiring Models: Predictive analytics can be used to identify candidates who are most likely to succeed in specific roles. By analyzing data from past hires, such as their qualifications, experience, and performance outcomes, HR can build models that predict the likelihood of a candidate's success. This helps reduce the risk of bad hires and improves overall recruitment efficiency.

Applicant Screening: Predictive analytics can streamline the applicant screening process by scoring candidates based on their likelihood of success. This allows HR teams to focus on the most promising candidates, saving time and resources during the recruitment process.

Employee Retention

Turnover Prediction: One of the most common applications of predictive analytics in HR is predicting employee turnover. By analyzing factors such as job satisfaction, engagement levels, compensation, and career progression, HR can identify employees who are at risk of leaving the organization. This allows for timely interventions, such as targeted retention initiatives or career development opportunities.

Retention Strategy Optimization: Predictive analytics can also help HR design more effective retention strategies by identifying the factors that most influence employee loyalty. For example, if data shows that employees are more likely to stay with the company if they receive regular professional development opportunities, HR can prioritize these initiatives.

Succession Planning through Predictive Models

Succession planning is a critical process for ensuring that an organization has the leadership talent needed to achieve its strategic goals and maintain business continuity. Traditionally, succession planning has relied on subjective assessments of potential leaders, often based on managerial opinions or past performance. However, the advent of predictive models has revolutionized this process, enabling organizations to make data-driven decisions that enhance the accuracy, fairness, and effectiveness of succession planning.

This chapter explores the role of predictive models in succession planning, including how they are developed, the benefits they offer, and the challenges involved in their implementation.

Key Components of Succession Planning Models

Data Collection: The foundation of any predictive model is high-quality data. For succession planning, relevant data includes performance evaluations, 360-degree feedback, training and development records, career progression, and behavioral assessments.

Variable Selection: The next step involves selecting the variables that will be included in the model. Common variables include leadership competencies, performance metrics, job tenure, education, and potential for growth. The selection of variables should align with the organization's leadership criteria and strategic goals.

Model Development: The predictive model is developed once the data is prepared and variables are selected. Techniques such as regression analysis, decision trees, and machine learning algorithms are commonly used to build models that predict leadership potential.

Validation and Testing: After the model is developed, it must be validated and tested to ensure its accuracy. This involves comparing the model's predictions with actual outcomes, making adjustments as needed to improve its reliability.

10.3. Types of Predictive Models for Succession Planning

Regression Models: These models predict leadership potential based on the relationship between dependent and independent variables. For example, a regression model might predict future leadership success based on variables like past performance scores, education level, and years of experience.

Decision Trees: Decision tree models segment data into branches based on decision rules derived from the data. In succession planning, a decision tree might classify employees into different categories based on their likelihood of success in leadership roles.

Machine Learning Models: More advanced machine learning models like random forests or neural networks can analyze large datasets and complex relationships between variables to predict leadership potential. These models are particularly useful for handling high-dimensional data and uncovering patterns that might not be evident through traditional statistical methods.

10.4. Applications of Predictive Models in Succession Planning

Identifying High-Potential Leaders

One of the primary applications of predictive models in succession planning is identifying high-potential employees who are well-suited for leadership roles. Predictive models can rank employees based on their likelihood of success in future leadership positions by analyzing data on performance, skills, and behavioral traits.

Assessing Readiness for Leadership Roles

Predictive models can also be used to assess an employee's readiness for leadership roles. This involves evaluating their current capabilities and their potential for growth and development. For example, an employee may have strong technical skills but may need further development in areas like strategic thinking or people management to be ready for a leadership role.

Planning for Leadership Gaps

Predictive models help organizations anticipate future leadership gaps by forecasting when key leaders are likely to retire or leave the organization. This allows HR to proactively develop and implement succession plans, ensuring qualified candidates are ready to step into leadership roles as needed.

Tailoring Development Programs

Another key application of predictive models is in tailoring leadership development programs to the needs of high-potential employees. Organizations can create personalized development plans that prepare them for future leadership roles by identifying specific areas where employees need development. This targeted approach ensures that employees receive the support they need to succeed.

10.5. The Future of Predictive Models in Succession Planning

Integration with Artificial Intelligence

The future of predictive models in succession planning will likely involve greater integration with artificial intelligence (AI). AI can enhance the accuracy and sophistication of predictive models, allowing for more precise forecasts of leadership potential and more tailored development plans.

Real-Time Succession Planning

As technology advances, predictive models may enable real-time succession planning, allowing organizations to respond immediately to changes in leadership needs. This will further enhance the agility and responsiveness of succession planning processes.

Ethical and Responsible Use

The future of predictive models in succession planning will also involve a greater focus on ethical and responsible use. Organizations will need to establish clear guidelines and practices to ensure that predictive models are used to respect employee rights, promote fairness, and support positive organizational outcomes.

Conclusion

Predictive models represent a powerful tool for enhancing succession planning, offering data-driven insights that improve leadership development efforts' accuracy, fairness, and effectiveness. Organizations can proactively identify and nurture future leaders by adopting predictive models, ensuring business continuity, aligning leadership with strategic goals, and supporting diversity and inclusion initiatives. However, the successful implementation of predictive models requires careful attention to data quality, ethical considerations, change management, and ongoing monitoring and refinement to maintain their relevance and accuracy.

10.6. Identifying High-Potential Employees with Data

High-potential employees, often referred to as "HiPos," are those individuals within an organization who demonstrate the capacity, commitment, and motivation to rise to and excel in more senior roles. Identifying these employees early allows organizations to invest in their development, preparing them for leadership and critical roles that are essential for the organization's future success. Traditionally, the identification of high-potential employees relied on subjective judgments and managerial assessments. However, the advent of data analytics has transformed this process, enabling a more objective, accurate, and comprehensive approach.

10.7. The Importance of Identifying High-Potential Employees

Strategic Talent Management

Identifying high-potential employees is crucial for strategic talent management. By recognizing and nurturing talent, organizations can build a robust leadership pipeline, ensuring that they are prepared to meet future challenges and achieve long-term objectives.

Enhancing Employee Engagement and Retention

When identified as high-potential, employees often receive more opportunities for growth and development, leading to increased engagement and job satisfaction. This, in turn, reduces turnover rates, as high-potential employees are more likely to stay with an organization that invests in their future.

Driving Organizational Performance

High-potential employees are typically high performers who can drive significant value for the organization. Organizations can enhance overall performance and achieve better business outcomes by placing them in key roles and providing them with the necessary support.

10.8. Leveraging Data to Identify High-Potential Employees

Types of Data Used

Performance Data: Historical performance reviews, key performance indicators (KPIs), and achievement records provide insights into an employee's past success and ability to deliver results.

Behavioral Data: Data from 360-degree feedback, peer reviews, and self-assessments helps in understanding an employee's behavioral traits, such as leadership potential, teamwork, and adaptability.

Developmental Data: Information on training and development programs completed, certifications earned, and skills acquired offers a view of an employee's commitment to personal and professional growth.

Engagement Data: Survey results, engagement scores, and participation in organizational activities can indicate an employee's alignment with the company's culture and their overall commitment.

Demographic and Psychometric Data: Age, tenure, education level, and psychometric test results can provide additional context for understanding an employee's potential, especially when combined with other data sources.

Data Collection Methods

HR Information Systems (HRIS): These systems capture and store vast amounts of employee data, including performance metrics, training records, and demographic information.

Employee Surveys: Regularly conducted surveys can provide insights into employee engagement, satisfaction, and perceived alignment with organizational values.

360-Degree Feedback: This comprehensive feedback mechanism involves collecting input from an employee's peers, subordinates, and supervisors, offering a well-rounded view of their potential.

Psychometric Assessments: These tests evaluate cognitive abilities, personality traits, and emotional intelligence, contributing to a deeper understanding of an employee's potential.

Analytical Techniques

Predictive Analytics: Using historical data and machine learning algorithms, predictive analytics can forecast which employees are most likely to succeed in more advanced roles based on past performance and other relevant factors.

Cluster Analysis: This technique groups employees with similar attributes or behaviors, helping to identify those who share characteristics with previously successful high-potential employees.

Regression Analysis: By analyzing the relationships between various factors (e.g., performance scores, engagement levels, development activities), regression analysis can help identify which variables are most predictive of high potential.

Talent Mapping: This involves creating visual representations of the data, such as matrices or heat maps, to highlight high-potential employees and track their development over time.

Conclusion

Identifying high-potential employees is critical for building a strong leadership pipeline and ensuring long-term organizational success. By leveraging data, organizations can enhance the accuracy, fairness, and effectiveness of this process, leading to better outcomes for both employees and the organization. However, it is essential to address challenges related to data quality, privacy, and ethical considerations, and to balance data-driven insights with human judgment. As technology continues to evolve, data-driven methods for identifying high-potential employees will become increasingly sophisticated, offering new opportunities for strategic talent management.

Part 11: Tools and Technologies for Data-Driven HR

Data-driven HR refers to the use of data and analytics to inform and enhance human resource management practices. By leveraging data, HR professionals can make more informed decisions, improve employee experiences, and align HR strategies with business objectives. Adopting data-driven HR requires using various tools and technologies that enable the collection, analysis, and application of HR data. This chapter explores the key tools and technologies that support data-driven HR, their functionalities, and how they contribute to effective human resource management.

11.1. Overview of HR Analytics Software

HR analytics, also known as people analytics or workforce analytics, involves systematically collecting, analyzing, and interpreting HR data to improve decision-making, predict trends, and enhance organizational outcomes. HR analytics software facilitates this process by providing tools for data management, statistical analysis, and reporting.

Data Integration

HR analytics software integrates data from various HR systems, such as HRIS, ATS, LMS, and employee engagement platforms. This creates a centralized data repository that provides a comprehensive view of the workforce, enabling more accurate analysis and reporting.

11.2. Advanced Analytics and Reporting

Descriptive Analytics: Provides insights into what has happened in the organization by analyzing historical data. This includes reports on employee turnover, hiring trends, and performance metrics.

Predictive Analytics: Uses statistical models and machine learning algorithms to predict future trends, such as turnover risk, employee performance, and potential leadership gaps.

Prescriptive Analytics: Recommends specific actions based on predictive insights. For example, if predictive analytics indicates a high turnover risk for a particular department, prescriptive analytics might suggest targeted employee retention interventions.

Dashboards and Data Visualization

HR analytics software often includes customizable dashboards that allow users to visualize data in various formats, such as charts, graphs, and heat maps. This makes it easier to interpret complex data and communicate insights to stakeholders.

Employee Surveys and Feedback Analysis

Some HR analytics software includes tools for conducting and analyzing employee surveys. These tools can track employee sentiment over time, identify areas of concern, and correlate feedback with other HR metrics, such as engagement and performance.

Talent Mapping and Succession Planning

HR analytics software can map out talent within the organization, identifying high-potential employees and assessing readiness for leadership roles. This feature supports succession planning by ensuring that the organization is prepared for future leadership transitions.

Benchmarking

Benchmarking features allow organizations to compare their HR metrics with industry standards or peer organizations. This helps identify areas where the organization excels or lags, informing strategic decisions and goal setting.

Conclusion

HR analytics software is vital for modern HR management, providing the data and insights needed to make informed decisions, optimize workforce planning, and align HR practices with organizational goals. While implementing HR analytics software presents challenges, the benefits far outweigh the difficulties, offering organizations a powerful means to enhance their HR strategies and drive business success. As technology continues to advance, HR analytics software will become even more integral to effective human resource management, offering new opportunities for innovation and growth.

Part 12: AI and Machine Learning in HR

Artificial Intelligence (AI) and Machine Learning (ML) are transforming various aspects of human resource management by automating tasks, enhancing decision-making, and providing deeper insights into workforce dynamics. These technologies are increasingly integrated into HR systems, enabling organizations to analyze vast amounts of data, predict trends, and implement more personalized and effective HR strategies. This chapter explores the role of AI and ML in HR, their applications, benefits, and the challenges associated with their adoption.

12.1. Understanding AI and Machine Learning

Definition of Artificial Intelligence and Machine Learning

Artificial Intelligence (AI): AI refers to the simulation of human intelligence in machines that are programmed to think, learn, and make decisions. In HR, AI can automate tasks, provide data-driven insights, and enhance employee experiences.

Machine Learning (ML): A subset of AI, ML involves the use of algorithms and statistical models that allow computers to learn from and make predictions or decisions based on data. In HR, ML can identify patterns in employee behavior, predict outcomes, and suggest actions.

12.2. Evolution of AI and ML in HR

AI and ML in HR have evolved from basic automation tools to sophisticated systems capable of predictive analytics, natural language processing, and even sentiment analysis. This evolution has enabled HR professionals to move from reactive to proactive and predictive management practices.

12.3. Benefits of AI and Machine Learning in HR

Increased Efficiency

AI and ML automate repetitive and time-consuming HR tasks, such as resume screening, scheduling interviews, and processing payroll. This frees up HR professionals to focus on more strategic activities, such as employee engagement and talent development.

Enhanced Decision-Making

AI and ML provide data-driven insights that enhance decision-making in HR. By analyzing vast amounts of data, these technologies help HR professionals make more informed decisions about hiring, performance management, and employee retention.

Improved Employee Experience

AI-powered tools can create more personalized and responsive HR processes, from tailored onboarding experiences to personalized learning and development programs. This leads to higher employee satisfaction and engagement.

Predictive Capabilities

ML algorithms can predict future outcomes based on historical data, enabling HR to anticipate and address potential issues before they become problems. This includes predicting employee turnover, identifying high-potential employees, and forecasting workforce needs.

Bias Reduction

AI can help reduce bias in HR processes by making decisions based on data rather than subjective judgments. This is particularly valuable in areas such as recruitment and performance reviews, where unconscious bias can influence decisions.

12.4. Future Trends in AI and Machine Learning in HR

AI-Driven Talent Management

The future of HR will see AI playing a central role in talent management, from identifying and developing high-potential employees to creating personalized career paths. AI will enable more proactive and strategic talent management practices, helping organizations to build and retain a competitive workforce.

Real-Time Employee Insights

As AI and ML technologies advance, HR teams will have access to real-time insights into employee behavior, engagement, and performance. This will allow for more agile and responsive HR management, with the ability to address issues as they arise.

Integration with Other Technologies

AI and ML will increasingly be integrated with other emerging technologies, such as blockchain and the Internet of Things (IoT), to provide even more comprehensive HR solutions. This could include enhanced employee tracking, secure data sharing, and advanced analytics capabilities.

Ethical AI in HR

As AI adoption grows, there will be a greater focus on ensuring that AI systems in HR are ethical, transparent, and aligned with organizational values. This will involve developing guidelines and best practices for the responsible use of AI in HR.

Conclusion

AI and Machine Learning are revolutionizing HR by automating processes, enhancing decision-making, and providing deeper insights into workforce dynamics. While there are challenges associated with their adoption, the benefits of AI and ML in HR are significant, offering the potential to transform how organizations manage their people. As these technologies continue to evolve, they will play an increasingly important role in shaping the future of HR, enabling more strategic, data-driven, and personalized approaches to human resource management.

Part 13: Case Studies of Data-Driven HR Success

Introduction to Data-Driven HR Success

The adoption of data-driven approaches in HR has enabled organizations to transform their human resource management practices, leading to improved decision-making, enhanced employee experiences, and better alignment with business objectives. This chapter presents a series of case studies from different industries that highlight how organizations have successfully implemented data-driven HR strategies, the challenges they faced, and the outcomes they achieved.

Case Study 1: Improving Employee Retention at TechCorp

Background

TechCorp, a rapidly growing technology company, faced a high employee turnover rate, particularly among its software developers. The company recognized that retaining top talent was crucial for maintaining its competitive edge and sought to leverage data-driven HR practices to address this challenge.

Approach

Data Collection: TechCorp began by gathering data from various sources, including exit interviews, employee surveys, performance reviews, and HRIS data. They focused on identifying patterns that could indicate the reasons behind employee turnover.

Predictive Analytics: The HR team implemented a predictive analytics model to identify employees at risk of leaving the company. The model analyzed factors such as tenure, performance ratings, engagement scores, and participation in development programs.

Targeted Interventions: Based on the insights from the predictive model, TechCorp introduced targeted retention initiatives. These included personalized career development plans, mentorship programs, and enhanced employee recognition efforts.

Challenges

Data Quality: One of the initial challenges was ensuring the accuracy and completeness of the data collected from various sources.

Employee Trust: There was some resistance from employees who were concerned about how their data would be used, necessitating transparent communication about the purpose and benefits of the initiative.

Outcomes

Reduced Turnover: Within a year of implementing the data-driven retention strategy, TechCorp saw a 15% reduction in turnover among its software developers.

Engagement: Employee engagement scores improved, particularly among those identified as at risk of leaving, due to the personalized development opportunities and increased recognition.

Business Impact: The reduction in turnover saved the company significant costs associated with recruiting and onboarding new employees, and helped maintain productivity in critical projects.

Case Study 2: Enhancing Diversity and Inclusion at GlobalBank

Background

GlobalBank, a leading financial services institution, recognized the need to enhance diversity and inclusion (D&I) within its workforce. Despite having various D&I initiatives in place, progress was slow, and the organization decided to take a data-driven approach to accelerate change.

Approach

Diversity Metrics: The HR team began by establishing clear metrics to track diversity across different dimensions, including gender, ethnicity, age, and career levels. They used data from HRIS, recruitment systems, and employee surveys.

AI-Powered Recruitment: GlobalBank implemented AI-driven recruitment tools designed to reduce bias in the hiring process. These tools analyzed job descriptions, candidate profiles, and hiring outcomes to ensure that decisions were based on qualifications rather than unconscious bias.

Inclusion Index: The organization developed an "Inclusion Index" based on employee feedback, measuring employees' perceptions of inclusion, fairness, and belonging within the company. This index was regularly monitored and reported to senior leadership.

Challenges

Bias in Data: One challenge was ensuring that the data used for decision-making did not inadvertently reinforce existing biases. The HR team worked closely with data scientists to validate the models and ensure fairness.

Sustaining Momentum: Maintaining momentum and engagement with D&I initiatives required continuous communication, training, and leadership commitment.

Outcomes

Increased Diversity: Within two years, GlobalBank saw a 20% increase in the diversity of its leadership team and a 10% increase in the overall diversity of its workforce.

Higher Inclusion Scores: The Inclusion Index showed a marked improvement, with more employees reporting a sense of belonging and fairness within the organization.

Recognition and Awards: GlobalBank received several industry awards for its D&I efforts, enhancing its reputation as an inclusive employer.

Case Study 3: Optimizing Workforce Planning at HealthPlus

Background

HealthPlus, a large healthcare provider, faced challenges with workforce planning, particularly in ensuring adequate staffing levels in its hospitals during peak periods. The organization struggled with balancing staff availability, patient demand, and budget constraints.

Approach

Data Integration: HealthPlus integrated data from various sources, including patient admission records, staffing schedules, and financial data, into a centralized HR analytics platform.

Predictive Workforce Analytics: The HR team used predictive analytics to forecast staffing needs based on historical patient data, seasonal trends, and external factors such as flu outbreaks.

Dynamic Scheduling: The insights from the predictive models were used to create dynamic staffing schedules that could be adjusted in real-time to meet changing demands. The system also recommended cross-training staff to fill multiple roles.

Challenges

Data Integration: Integrating data from disparate systems was a significant challenge that required substantial IT resources and collaboration between HR, IT, and operational departments.

Staff Flexibility: Ensuring staff were flexible and willing to adapt to dynamic schedules required clear communication and incentives, such as shift differentials and cross-training opportunities.

Outcomes

Improved Staffing Efficiency: HealthPlus achieved a 25% improvement in staffing efficiency, reducing both understaffing and overstaffing during critical periods.

Cost Savings: The optimized staffing schedules resulted in significant cost savings, as the organization reduced the need for expensive temporary staffing and overtime.

Enhanced Patient Care: By ensuring that staffing levels matched patient demand, HealthPlus improved patient care outcomes, including reduced wait times and higher patient satisfaction scores.

Case Study 4: Driving Employee Engagement at RetailX

Background

RetailX, a major retail chain, struggled with low employee engagement, which was affecting customer service and overall business performance. The company decided to implement a data-driven approach to identify and address the root causes of disengagement.

Approach

Employee Sentiment Analysis: RetailX utilized AI-powered tools to analyze employee feedback from surveys, emails, and social media posts. The goal was to identify common themes and sentiments related to engagement.

Engagement Drivers: The HR team conducted a deep dive into the data to identify the key drivers of engagement, such as work-life balance, career development opportunities, and management support.

Targeted Initiatives: Based on the insights, RetailX introduced targeted initiatives, including flexible work arrangements, leadership development programs, and enhanced recognition systems.

Challenges

Data Privacy Concerns: Employees were initially wary of how their feedback would be used, raising concerns about privacy and potential repercussions.

Change Management: Implementing new engagement initiatives required significant change management efforts, particularly in changing leadership behaviors and expectations.

Outcomes

Increased Engagement Scores: Within 18 months, RetailX saw a significant increase in employee engagement scores, particularly in areas related to work-life balance and management support.

Improved Customer Satisfaction: As employee engagement improved, so did customer satisfaction scores, leading to increased sales and repeat business.

Reduced Turnover: The company also experienced a decrease in turnover, particularly among frontline employees, who were more engaged and motivated.

Conclusion

These case studies illustrate the power of data-driven HR practices in addressing a wide range of challenges, from employee retention and diversity to workforce planning and engagement. By leveraging data and analytics, organizations can make more informed decisions, implement more effective HR strategies, and ultimately achieve better business outcomes. While the journey to becoming data-driven can present challenges, the rewards are substantial, offering organizations the tools they need to thrive in an increasingly competitive and complex business environment.

Part 14: Future Trends in Data-Driven HR

As the landscape of work continues to evolve, so too does the field of human resource management. Data-driven HR is at the forefront of this transformation, enabling organizations to harness the power of data and technology to drive more informed decisions, enhance employee experiences, and achieve strategic goals. This chapter explores the emerging trends that are shaping the future of data-driven HR, offering insights into how organizations can stay ahead of the curve.

The Integration of Emerging Technologies

Blockchain in HR

Blockchain technology will likely play a growing role in HR, particularly in areas such as employee verification, secure data sharing, and contract management. Blockchain's decentralized nature can enhance transparency and trust in HR processes.

Example: Blockchain could be used to verify credentials during the hiring process, ensuring the accuracy and authenticity of candidates' qualifications.

Virtual and Augmented Reality in HR

Virtual Reality (VR) and Augmented Reality (AR) will become more integrated into HR practices, particularly in training, onboarding, and remote work. These technologies can create immersive learning environments and enhance collaboration among geographically dispersed teams.

Example: VR could be used to simulate real-world scenarios for training purposes, allowing employees to practice skills in a controlled, risk-free environment.

Conclusion

The future of data-driven HR is one of innovation, agility, and personalization. As technologies like AI, machine learning, and blockchain continue to evolve, they will offer unprecedented opportunities for HR professionals to enhance their practices and drive organizational success. However, with these advancements come new challenges, particularly around ethics, privacy, and the responsible use of data. By staying ahead of these trends and adopting a forward-thinking approach, organizations can ensure they are well-positioned to thrive in the rapidly changing world of work.

Students Take away

A data-driven HR strategy empowers organizations to make informed decisions by leveraging data and analytics. HR teams can use data to assess employee performance, engagement, and turnover to identify trends, optimize recruitment, and tailor development programs. It allows HR professionals to predict workforce needs, improve talent retention, and enhance overall productivity. Data-driven insights also help create personalized employee experiences, increasing satisfaction and engagement. Ultimately, this approach enables HR to align its strategy with business goals, making it more proactive and effective in managing people and driving organizational success.

Glossary of Key Terms in Data-Driven HR

I. AI-Powered Recruitment

II. An approach to hiring that utilizes artificial intelligence to automate and enhance various aspects of the recruitment process, including candidate sourcing, resume screening, and interview scheduling. AI-powered recruitment aims to reduce bias, increase efficiency, and improve the quality of hires.

III. Agile Workforce Planning

IV. A dynamic approach to workforce planning that allows organizations to quickly adapt their workforce strategies in response to changing market conditions, business needs, and external disruptions. Agile workforce planning emphasizes flexibility and responsiveness.

V. Analytics Platform

VI. A software solution that integrates and analyzes data from multiple sources, providing insights and visualizations to support data-driven decision-making in HR and other business areas.

VII. Autonomous HR Systems

VIII. HR systems that leverage artificial intelligence and automation to perform routine tasks without human intervention. Examples include automated onboarding processes, benefits administration, and employee performance evaluations.

IX. Big Data

X. Large volumes of data generated from various sources, such as employee records, social media, and business transactions. In HR, big data is used to uncover patterns, trends, and insights that can inform strategic decision-making.

XI. Blockchain in HR

XII. The use of blockchain technology to enhance transparency, security, and trust in HR processes. Applications of blockchain in HR include verifying employee credentials, managing contracts, and ensuring secure data sharing.

XIII. Crowdsourcing HR Solutions

XIV. The practice of gathering ideas, feedback, and solutions from a broad group of employees or external stakeholders. Crowdsourcing is used in HR to develop more inclusive and innovative policies, programs, and strategies.

XV. Data Democratization

XVI. The process of making data and analytics tools accessible to a broader range of employees, beyond just data specialists. In HR, data democratization enables managers and employees to make more informed decisions based on real-time data insights.

XVII. Data-Driven HR

XVIII. An approach to human resource management that relies on data analysis and metrics to inform decisions, strategies, and processes. Data-driven HR seeks to optimize workforce performance, enhance employee experience, and align HR practices with organizational goals.

XIX. Employee Experience (EX)

XX. The overall perception and feelings that employees have about their interactions with an organization, including aspects such as work environment, culture, benefits, and career development opportunities. Data-driven HR uses analytics to personalize and improve the employee experience.

XXI. Employee Sentiment Analysis

XXII. The use of AI and natural language processing (NLP) to analyze employee feedback, such as survey responses or social media posts, to gauge employee emotions, opinions, and overall sentiment. Sentiment analysis helps organizations understand and respond to employee concerns.

XXIII. Ethical AI in HR

XXIV. The practice of ensuring that AI technologies used in HR are applied in a manner that is fair, transparent, and aligned with ethical standards. This includes addressing biases in AI algorithms and ensuring that decisions made by AI are equitable.

XXV. HR Analytics

XXVI. The application of data analysis techniques to human resource data to gain insights into workforce trends, employee behavior, and organizational performance. HR analytics supports evidence-based decision-making in areas such as recruitment, retention, and employee development.

XXVII. Inclusion Index

XXVIII. A metric used to measure employees' perceptions of inclusion, fairness, and belonging within an organization. The Inclusion Index is often derived from employee surveys and is used to assess the effectiveness of diversity and inclusion initiatives.

XXIX. Machine Learning (ML) in HR

XXX. A subset of artificial intelligence that involves the use of algorithms and statistical models to analyze data and make predictions or decisions without explicit programming. In HR, machine learning is used for tasks such as predictive analytics, employee sentiment analysis, and workforce planning.

XXXI. People Analytics

XXXII. A data-driven approach to managing and improving workforce performance by analyzing data on employees' behavior, performance, and engagement. People analytics helps organizations make informed decisions about talent management, leadership development, and employee retention.

XXXIII. Predictive Analytics in HR

XXXIV. The use of statistical models and machine learning algorithms to analyze historical HR data and predict future outcomes. Predictive analytics in HR can forecast employee turnover, identify high-potential employees, and optimize workforce planning.

XXXV. Real-Time Employee Feedback

XXXVI. The collection and analysis of employee feedback as it is provided, often through pulse surveys or digital platforms. Real-time feedback allows organizations to quickly identify and address issues, enhancing employee engagement and satisfaction.

XXXVII. Skills-Based Talent Management

XXXVIII. An approach to talent management that focuses on identifying, developing, and utilizing employees' skills to meet current and future organizational needs. This approach is increasingly data-driven, using analytics to match skills with job roles and development opportunities.

XXXIX. Talent Analytics

XL. The practice of applying data analysis to talent management processes, such as recruitment, development, and retention. Talent analytics helps organizations make data-driven decisions about hiring, promoting, and developing employees.

XLI. Virtual Reality (VR) in HR

XLII. The use of virtual reality technology to create immersive simulations for training, onboarding, and other HR activities. VR allows employees to practice skills and scenarios in a controlled, realistic environment.

XLIII. Well-Being Analytics

XLIV. The use of data to monitor and improve the physical, mental, and emotional well-being of employees. Well-being analytics tracks factors such as stress levels, workload balance, and overall satisfaction to support employee health and productivity.

Chapter 6: Fundamentals Of Critical Thinking

Part 1: Introduction

This topic helps to learn the ways to enhance cognitive abilities. It refines thinkers' intellect, clarify their reasoning, and assist them in making more informed choices. Critical way of thinking will guide any individual—methodically—on how to dissect problems, reason coherently, and present arguments persuasively. The commitment, this topic will cultivate is towards understanding the analytical and reasoning skills essential for success in academia and corporate world of profession, and life in general. Critical thinking is the cornerstone of the overall experience. The purpose of education is not merely to fill students with information; rather, it is to equip them with the ability to think critically. This section is specifically crafted to achieve that goal. It will aid learner in acquiring the skills and mindset necessary to become an autonomous, self-motivated thinker and performer. Engaging in critical thinking is a journey. Achieving mental acuity requires significant effort. Moreover, exercising independent thought can sometimes be daunting. However, ultimately, the outcome will emerge as a more intelligent, resilient, and self-assured thinker.

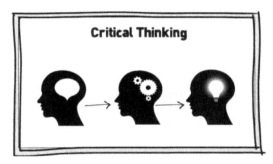

The term "critical" also refers to the application of skilled judgment or observation. In this context, critical thinking encompasses the ability to think clearly and intelligently. More specifically, critical thinking is a broad term that encompasses various cognitive skills and intellectual attitudes essential for effectively identifying, analysing, and evaluating arguments and claims of truth. It involves recognizing and addressing personal biases and preconceptions, formulating and articulating persuasive reasons to support conclusions, and making rational, informed decisions regarding beliefs and actions.

1.1 What is Critical Thinking?

This may be stated that Critical thinking involves a conscious awareness of the decisions people undertake. To gain a deeper understanding of this concept, it is beneficial to examine the underlying reasons for individual's decision-making processes. Majority of our decisions are influenced by three primary stressors: Physical stress, Emotional stress, Material/financial stress respectively. Critical thinking represents a disciplined approach to analysing any subject, issue, or content. It engages in thoughtful consideration and subsequently applies these intellectual insights. A significant advantage of critical thinking is its ability to increase level of the quality of reasoning skills. This mode of thinking is characterized by intellectual virtues such as clarity, sound evidence, precision, logical reasoning, relevance, consistency, depth, breadth, and fairness.

1.2 How to Develop Critical Thinking?

The numerous benefits of critical thinking reach well beyond academic settings. To begin with, critical thinking enhances decision-making capabilities by providing individuals with the necessary tools to evaluate options, consider potential outcomes, and make more informed choices. Additionally, those who engage in critical thinking experience increased self-reflection, leading to a deeper awareness of their own biases and areas for growth.

Individuals who think critically become knowledgeable participants in society, capable of navigating the vast array of information with discernment, effectively distinguishing between credible sources and misinformation. Moreover, this essential skill promotes creative problem-solving, enabling individuals to devise innovative solutions to complex issues. Among the key advantages of critical thinking are:

Improved decision-making Critical thinkers are adept at analysing the advantages and disadvantages, exploring alternatives, and predicting possible outcomes. This results in more informed and effective decision-making in both personal and professional contexts.

Enhanced self-reflection By cultivating a practice of introspection, critical thinkers develop greater self-awareness, allowing them to identify their own biases and limitations. This increased self-awareness facilitates ongoing improvement and adaptation in their thought processes.

Being well-informed Critical thinkers actively pursue a variety of information sources, ensuring a well-rounded understanding of intricate issues. This equips them to participate in meaningful discussions and make constructive contributions to their communities.

The capacity to recognize misinformation In an era rife with misinformation, critical thinkers are equipped to differentiate between fact and falsehood. They critically evaluate sources, verify information, and remain vigilant against misleading content.

Development of creative problem-solving skills Critical thinking fosters innovative and unconventional approaches to problem-solving. By examining multiple perspectives and questioning established norms, critical thinkers generate original solutions to challenging problematic situations for overcoming and thrive for better outcomes.

1.3 What are the benefits of Critical Thinking?

After examining some of the fundamental intellectual standards that guide critical reasoning, such as clarity and precision, it is pertinent to explore the specific benefits one can derive from a course in critical thinking. Upon entering college, students often find it surprising that their professors prioritize the robustness of their beliefs over the processes by which those beliefs were formed. The emphasis in higher education is placed on advanced cognitive skills, which involve the thoughtful and analytical assessment of ideas and information. Consequently, critical thinking is essential across the entire college curriculum. In a critical thinking course, students acquire a range of competencies that can significantly enhance their academic performance. These competencies encompass:

- comprehending the arguments and perspectives of others

- critically assessing those arguments and perspectives

- formulating and substantiating one's own well-founded arguments and perspectives.

Research indicates that less than half of contemporary college graduates anticipate working in their chosen field within five years post-graduation. This statistic highlights the evolving dynamics of the job market. Employers are increasingly seeking individuals who possess strong thinking and communication abilities rather than those with narrowly defined technical skills, which are often best acquired through practical experience. They value quick learners capable of problem-solving, creative thinking, information gathering and analysis, drawing sound conclusions from data, and articulating their ideas clearly and effectively. These are precisely the generalized thinking and problem-solving abilities that a critical thinking course is designed to enhance.

Critical thinking holds significant importance in various situations beyond the educational and professional environments. Let us examine three key areas where this is evident. Firstly, critical thinking aids individuals in steering clear of unwise personal choices. At some point, everyone has made decisions regarding purchases, relationships, or personal conduct that they later recognized as misguided or irrational. By fostering a more careful, clear, and logical approach to significant life choices, critical thinking can help mitigate such errors. Secondly, critical thinking is essential in enhancing democratic practices. Contrary to the views of skeptics, it is indeed "we the people" who ultimately determine governance and its objectives in a democracy. Thus, it is crucial for citizens to make decisions that are well-informed and thoughtfully considered. Many pressing societal issues—such as environmental degradation, nuclear threats, religious and ethnic intolerance, deteriorating urban areas, failing educational systems, and escalating healthcare expenses—can be attributed to inadequate critical thinking. As Albert Einstein aptly stated, "The significant problems we face cannot be solved at the level of thinking we were at when we created them."

Critical thinking merits attention for its intrinsic value, particularly in terms of the personal growth it fosters in our lives. A fundamental aspect of the human experience is that the majority of individuals tend to accept information at face value. Historically, many have uncritically accepted notions such as the earth being the center of the universe, the belief that diseases were caused by demons, the justification of slavery, and the perception of women as inferior to men. Engaging in critical thinking, with honesty and bravery, can liberate us from the unexamined beliefs and biases instilled by our upbringing and societal influences. It enables us to distance ourselves from the dominant customs and ideologies of our culture, prompting us to question, "What I have been taught—does it hold true?" In essence, critical thinking empowers us to lead self-reflective and examined lives. This form of personal emancipation is, as the term suggests, the paramount objective of a liberal arts education. Beyond its various advantages, a liberal education offers no greater reward than this.

1.4 What are the barriers to Critical Thinking?

What are the prevalent obstacles to engaging in critical and analytical thinking? Several of these challenges were illustrated in the visual summary, including:

- **Misinterpretation** This may occur due to variations in language or culture, insufficient understanding of the underlying 'processes,' or the misconception that critical thinking equates to making 'negative' remarks.

- **Hesitance** to question established norms or authorities within a discipline and to explore alternative perspectives, often stemming from discomfort or fear of making mistakes.

- **Insufficient depth of knowledge**. A lack of comprehensive understanding, often resulting from not having thoroughly explored the subject matter.

As a critical and reflective thinker, it is essential to recognize the obstacles anyone may encounter, acknowledge the difficulties they present, and strive to navigate them effectively. This process begins with a clear understanding of expectations. Many experience apprehension when it comes to questioning the work of established experts. However, critical thinking does not equate to disputing someone's work or asserting their incorrectness; rather, it promotes a deeper comprehension, the exploration of alternative perspectives, and active engagement in thought, discussion, or research that contributes to your independent judgment. At the advanced level, it is also imperative to engage in extensive reading on a subject to effectively participate in critical and analytical thinking and to formulate inquiries: there are no definitive 'right' or 'wrong' answers, only well-supported arguments.

1.5 Key Takeaways

Critical thinking is the cornerstone of the overall experience. The purpose of education is not merely to fill students with information; rather, it is to equip them with the ability to think critically. This section is specifically crafted to achieve that goal. It will aid learner in acquiring the skills and mindset necessary to become an autonomous, self-motivated thinker and performer. Critical Thinking engage in leadership training initiatives aimed at refining critical competencies such as communication, decision-making, problem-solving, strategic thinking, and emotional intelligence.

Part 2: Learning to Recognize Arguments

2.1. What is an Argument?

When individuals encounter the term "argument," they often associate it with a dispute or a heated exchange. In the realm of critical thinking, however, an argument is defined as a claim that is supported by reasons. Arguments consist of one or more premises along with a conclusion. The premises serve as statements within the argument that provide evidence or rationale for accepting another statement, known as the conclusion. The conclusion represents the assertion that the premises aim to substantiate or validate. Thus, an argument is essentially a collection of statements, where one or more (referred to as premises) are designed to support or prove another statement (identified as the conclusion). A statement is defined as a sentence that can be categorized as either true or false. For instance, consider the following examples of statements: Red is a place. God does not exist. Abortion is morally wrong. Men don't cry etc. Some of these statements are evidently true, others are clearly false, and some are subject to debate. Nonetheless, each qualifies as a statement since each can be introduced with the phrases "It is true " or "It is false."

2.2. Importance of Identifying Arguments

It is essential to keep in mind three key aspects:

➤ **Arguments consist of statements.**

➤ **They culminate in a conclusion.**

➤ **They include at least one premise.**

Arguments are composed of statements, which are declarative sentences. Unlike questions or commands, statements possess a truth value. They assert that the world is in a specific state; questions do not make such assertions. For instance, if someone inquired about your activities after dinner the previous evening, you would not accuse them of dishonesty. A statement is deemed true when the world aligns with what it asserts; conversely, if it does not, the statement is considered false. Within an argument, one of the statements is designated as the conclusion. This conclusion represents the assertion that is meant to be substantiated. Take the following argument as an example: Calculus II will not be more challenging than Calculus I. Jyoti performed well in Calculus I. Therefore, Jyoti is likely to excel in Calculus II. In this case, the conclusion is that Jyoti is likely to excel in Calculus II, while the other two statements serve as premises. Premises provide the rationale for believing the conclusion to be true.

To facilitate the evaluation of the argument, it will present that in what is referred to as "**standard form.**" This involves listing each premise on a separate, numbered line. Following the last premise, a line will be drawn, and the conclusion will be written beneath it. 1. Calculus II will not be more difficult than Calculus I. 2. Jyoti performed well in Calculus I. 3. Therefore, Jyoti is likely to perform well in Calculus II. With the argument now structured in standard form, we can discuss premise 1, premise 2, and ensure that we are all referencing the same points clearly.

It is unfortunate that individuals seldom present their arguments in a standard format. Consequently, we must determine which statement serves as the conclusion and which one's function as premises. One should not assume that the conclusion is always positioned at the end of the argument. In fact, the conclusion may often appear at the beginning or even in the middle of the discourse. A more effective method for identifying premises and conclusions is to search for **indicator words**. These words serve as signals that the statement following them is either a premise or a conclusion. For instance, the example provided utilized a common indicator word for conclusions, namely 'so.' Another frequently used indicator for conclusions is 'therefore.'

Each argument is expected to utilize a single indicator word or phrase. Typically, when the conclusion appears at the end, it is introduced by a conclusion indicator. Consequently, all other statements serve as premises. Conversely, if the conclusion is presented at the beginning, the subsequent sentence is generally introduced by a premise indicator, with all following sentences also functioning as premises.

From the previous example Jyoti is likely to perform successfully in Calculus II, as it is expected to be no more challenging than Calculus I, in which she excelled. 2. It is anticipated that Jyoti will succeed in Calculus II, given that it should not present greater difficulties than Calculus I, where she demonstrated strong performance.

Another example Pug is classified as a mammal. Since all dogs belong to the category of mammals and Pug is identified as a dog, it follows that Pug is a mammal. The initial statement is a logical conclusion derived from the preceding premises. This reasoning assumes that the individual presenting the argument is both rational and logical, an assumption that may not necessarily hold true.

A significant challenge in our endeavour to identify arguments arises from the presence of numerous passages that may appear to be arguments but do not actually qualify as such.

The most prevalent categories include:

a) **Explanations** To ascertain whether a phrase serves as an explanation or an argument, begin by identifying the statement that appears to be the conclusion. Subsequently, consider whether it is reasonable to assume that the majority of individuals already accept that statement as true. If the response to this inquiry is affirmative, then the passage can be classified as an explanation.

b) **Simple assertions** do not constitute arguments. For instance, if a professor states that you will not receive an A in her course this semester without providing any justification, she has not presented an argument. This lack of reasoning means there are no grounds to accept the truth of her statement. Without premises, an argument cannot exist.

c) **Conditional statements** are structured as "If…, then…." They propose that if one condition holds true, another condition will also hold true. For example, consider the statement, "If you possess the winning lottery ticket, then you will receive ten lakhs." The assertion does not claim that you possess the winning ticket or that you will win the money; rather, it asserts the truth of the entire conditional statement. While conditionals can serve as premises or conclusions within arguments, they do not qualify as arguments in isolation.

d) **Loosely related statements** This morning, I awoke, proceeded to take a shower, and dressed myself. Following breakfast, I dedicated time to working on chapter 2 of the critical thinking text. Subsequently, I took a break and enjoyed another cup of coffee. While this may serve as a narrative of my day, it does not constitute an argument. The text lacks any elements that function as premises or a conclusion. It does not seek to establish proof for any assertion. It is essential to note that an argument must include a conclusion, presenting a statement that requires validation. In the absence of such a component, it cannot be classified as an argument, regardless of its superficial appearance.

2.3. Evaluating Arguments an Overview

The initial phase of assessing an argument involves identifying its type. Arguments are primarily classified as either deductive or inductive, based on their intended objectives. In deductive arguments, the premises are designed to definitively confirm the truth of the conclusion. Conversely, in inductive arguments, the premises aim to support the conclusion's probable truth rather than its certainty. Our primary focus will be on deductive arguments initially, with a subsequent exploration of inductive arguments in later sections. After confirming that an argument is deductive, the next step is to evaluate its validity. An argument is deemed valid when there exists a specific logical connection between the premises and the conclusion, such that if the premises hold true, the conclusion must also be true. This can be articulated as follows: Valid An argument is valid if and only if it is impossible for the premises to be true while the conclusion is false. Invalid An argument is invalid if and only if it does not meet the criteria for validity. It is important to note that asserting an argument's validity does not equate to asserting that it has a true conclusion or that its premises are true. To claim an argument is valid simply means that, assuming the premises are true, they would suffice to ensure the truth of the conclusion. If the argument is valid, and has all true premises, then it is a sound argument. Sound arguments always have true conclusions.

A deductively valid argument is characterized by having all true premises. Inductive arguments, by their nature, cannot be classified as valid, as their premises only suggest the likelihood of the conclusion being true. Therefore, we assess inductive arguments based on their strength. A strong inductive argument is one where the truth of the premises genuinely supports the probable truth of the conclusion. Conversely, an argument is deemed weak if the premises do not sufficiently establish the probable truth of the conclusion. It is essential to distinguish between valid/invalid and strong/weak arguments. An argument that is not valid is classified as invalid. These two categories are mutually exclusive and collectively exhaustive. It is impossible for one valid argument to be more valid than another; validity is an absolute condition. In contrast, inductive strength exists on a spectrum. A strong inductive argument can be further strengthened by adding additional premises. Increased evidence can enhance the likelihood of the conclusion being true. However, a valid argument cannot be made more valid by introducing another premise. The reason for this is that if an argument is valid, the premises already provide a complete assurance of the conclusion's truth. Adding another premise would not enhance this guarantee; if it did, it would imply that the original guarantee was not absolute, thereby questioning the validity of the initial argument.

Counterexamples serve as valuable tools for illustrating the invalidity of arguments. However, it is important to remember that the counterexample method cannot establish validity. If an argument is indeed valid, it will be impossible to present a counterexample against it. Conversely, the inability to produce a counterexample does not necessarily confirm the argument's validity; it may simply indicate a lack of creativity in the attempt.

2.4. Finding the Conclusion of an Argument

Identify the primary issue and consider the stance that the individual adopts regarding that issue.

- Examine the introduction or conclusion of the text; the main argument is frequently located in one of these sections.

- Reflect on the question, "What is the subject attempting to demonstrate?" This inquiry will lead you to the conclusion.

- Experiment with the word "therefore" preceding one of the assertions. If it aligns logically, that assertion is likely the conclusion.

- Utilize the "because" technique by attempting to appropriately complete the following statement: The subject asserts (conclusion) because (premise). The conclusion will typically precede the term "because."

2.5. What is not an Argument?

Arguments are prevalent in various aspects of our daily lives, including educational settings, workplaces, advertisements in magazines, editorials in newspapers, political debates, television documentaries, and radio talk shows. However, language serves purposes beyond merely presenting arguments; it is also employed to convey humor, perform songs, recite poetry, express emotions, report occurrences, pose inquiries, provide clarifications, offer prayers, issue commands, and exchange vows during weddings. This raises the question: how can we differentiate arguments from non-arguments? The fundamental criterion is straightforward. A set of statements qualifies as an argument when

(1) it consists of two or more statements and

(2) one of those statements (the conclusion) is asserted or intended to be substantiated by the others (the premises).

By utilizing this basic criterion, we can typically determine whether a specific passage constitutes an argument. Next, we will examine five categories of non-argumentative discourse that are often mistaken for arguments: • reports • unsupported assertions • conditional statements • illustrations • explanations.

2.6. Key Takeaways

An argument consists of a collection of statements, with one serving as the conclusion and the others as premises. The conclusion represents the assertion that the argument seeks to establish as true. The premises provide the rationale for accepting the conclusion as valid. It is important to note that explanations, conditional statements, and simple assertions do not qualify as arguments. Deductive reasoning aims to ensure the conclusion's truth with absolute certainty, while inductive reasoning seeks to demonstrate that the conclusion is likely to be true. In a valid argument, it is impossible for the premises to hold true while the conclusion is false. Conversely, in an invalid argument, the premises can be true even if the conclusion is false. A sound argument is characterized by its validity and the truth of all its premises. An inductively strong argument is one where the truth of the premises lends significant support to the conclusion's truth. In contrast, an inductively weak argument fails to provide sufficient support for the conclusion's probable truth. A counterexample serves as a coherent scenario where the premises of an argument are true, yet the conclusion is false, thereby demonstrating the deductive invalidity of the argument.

Part 3: Basic Logical Concepts

3.1. Deduction & Induction

In order to assess an argument effectively, it is essential to comprehend the nature of the argument being presented. Traditionally, arguments are categorized into two distinct types: deductive and inductive arguments. Given that the criteria for evaluating these two types differ significantly, it is crucial to recognize the distinctions between them. All arguments purport to offer support—namely, evidence or reasoning—for their conclusions. However, the extent of support claimed by different arguments varies considerably. Deductive arguments aim to establish their conclusions through strict, unavoidable logic, while inductive arguments seek to demonstrate that their conclusions are plausible or likely based on the provided premises.

Consider the following examples of deductive arguments:

1. All humans are mortal.

2. Arya Bhatt is human.

3. Therefore, Arya Bhatt is mortal.

If the president resides in the Rashtrapati Bhavan, then that is located in New Delhi.

2. The president does indeed reside in the Rashtrapati Bhavan.

3. Therefore, the president is located in New Delhi. It is evident that the conclusions of these arguments derive from the premises through a form of unavoidable logic. The conclusions of deductive arguments necessarily follow from their premises, as the premises are designed to furnish this level of rigorous, unassailable logical support for the conclusions.

Deductive arguments assert that they offer logically definitive support for their conclusions. In other words, they seek to demonstrate that their conclusions necessarily follow from the premises presented. Conversely, inductive arguments maintain that their conclusions are merely likely or probable based on the premises provided.

3.2. Reasoning

Deductive reasoning is defined by the following characteristics:

• It leads to necessary conclusions. If the premises of the argument are accurate—though it is important to note that they may not be—then the conclusion must be true without exception. There is no possibility for alternative interpretations.

• It combines a general assertion regarding a group with a statement identifying a member of that group, subsequently drawing a conclusion about that specific member. For instance, the premises in the liver argument are: Grilled liver invariably tastes like rubber, and this is grilled liver. Therefore, my conclusion is that this will also taste like rubber.

• It integrates a general prediction with a statement concerning a specific situation, allowing for a conclusion to be drawn. The premises clarify what is known about a particular cause-and-effect relationship, which are then utilized to infer conclusions about the situation. For example: If one consumes milk, it will induce sleepiness. You are not experiencing feeling sleepy. Hence, it can be concluded that you have not consumed milk.

Inductive reasoning is defined by several key characteristics:

• It typically relies on observation. The premises of inductive arguments are often fragments of evidence collected through either direct or indirect observation.

- The conclusions drawn are generally tentative generalizations regarding groups or relationships, as well as predictions. For instance, if one encounters a single spoiled fruit, one might conclude that all fruits of that type are similarly spoiled. If a small orange causes stomach discomfort, one may infer that all oranges will cause similar issues. Although these conclusions may appear to be established facts, they are based solely on observed instances, which means the complete picture may not be fully understood. Thus, while inductive conclusions may seem robust, they do not necessarily derive logically from the premises, and alternative conclusions, though perhaps less reasonable, remain a possibility.

3.3. Scientific Way

Scientific reasoning involves fundamental reasoning and problem-solving skills, incorporating essential inference processes for hypothesis formation, experimental design to test these hypotheses, differentiation between definitive and ambiguous evidence, and the interpretation of results as supportive or contradictory to the hypotheses. Despite numerous studies indicating that older children and even non-experts struggle with scientific reasoning (Kuhn et al., 1995; Schauble, 1996), recent research has highlighted early competencies in this area. Legare (2012) conducted experiments with children aged 2 to 6, asking them to determine why certain blocks activated the "blicket detector" while others did not. The study particularly focused on the relationship between the children's explanations and their exploratory actions with the blocks and device. It was found that the explanations provided by four- to six-year-olds influenced and directed their exploratory behaviour, which subsequently led to the modification and creation of new hypotheses. These results suggest that preschoolers possess the capability to test the hypotheses articulated in their explanations, showcasing early skills in hypothesis-testing activities. Additional research has also shown that preschoolers are capable of utilizing evidence to assess simple causal relationships (Gopnik et al., 2001).

Critical thinking and scientific reasoning represent distinct yet related constructs that encompass various higher-order cognitive processes, metacognitive strategies, and dispositions essential for interpreting information. Critical thinking is typically regarded as a more comprehensive construct (Holyoak and Morrison, 2005), incorporating a diverse range of cognitive processes and dispositions that are utilized variably in daily life and across different fields of inquiry, including the natural sciences, social sciences, and humanities. In contrast, scientific reasoning can be viewed as a specific subset of critical-thinking skills (comprising both cognitive and metacognitive processes and dispositions) that

1) facilitate the interpretation of information within scientific contexts and

2) reinforce the epistemological commitment to scientific methodologies and paradigms. Despite a longstanding emphasis in higher education on fostering critical thinking and reasoning as general or "transferable" skills, research increasingly supports the notion that reasoning and critical thinking are also contextually or domain-specific (Beyer et al., 2013). Some scholars, such as Lawson (2010), propose frameworks that explicitly define scientific reasoning in relation to critical-thinking skills. Nevertheless, there remains a scarcity of coherent frameworks and empirical evidence concerning the

general or domain-specific interconnections between scientific reasoning, as broadly defined, and critical-thinking skills.

3.4. Critical Reasoning

Critical reasoning involves the systematic identification, analysis, and resolution of problems. Key topics within critical reasoning include Statement and Argument, Statement and Assumption, Statement and Conclusion, Statement and Course of Action, as well as Cause and Effect, among others. Having established a clear understanding of the concept of critical reasoning, we will now explore the different types of critical reasoning that exist.

Various Forms of Critical Reasoning It is essential to explore the different forms of Critical Reasoning. Below is a detailed examination of each type:

1. Statement and Argument This category of critical reasoning questions presents a series of statements that articulate a particular viewpoint, showcasing differing opinions for or against a specific issue. Candidates are required to identify the most valid argument from the options provided.

2. Statement and Assumption In this type of critical reasoning question, candidates must analyse the given statements to arrive at an appropriate decision. This entails selecting the correct assumption based on the information presented.

3. Statement and Conclusion These critical reasoning questions consist of passages or statements followed by several conclusions. Candidates must evaluate the statements and determine which conclusion accurately follows from the provided information.

4. Statement and Course of Action In this type of critical reasoning question, a scenario is presented as a statement, accompanied by potential courses of action relevant to that scenario. Candidates are tasked with identifying which course of action should be pursued based on the information given.

5. Cause and Effect This category of critical reasoning questions involves two statements, and candidates must ascertain whether these statements represent independent causes, effects of a common cause, or merely a shared cause.

3.5. Key Takeaways

Critical thinking is characterized as the capacity to think with clarity and logic, recognizing the relationships among various concepts. Fundamentally, it necessitates that individuals employ their skills to uncover the rationale behind different phenomena. Active engagement in the learning process, as opposed to merely absorbing information, is a hallmark of effective critical reasoning. A proficient critical thinker will challenge ideas and assumptions instead of passively accepting them. They consistently strive to ascertain whether the ideas, arguments, and conclusions presented provide a comprehensive understanding of the subject matter at hand.

Part 4: Battle Of Bias

4.1. Strengthen Critical Thinking

In the contemporary digital landscape, navigating through an overwhelming amount of information to uncover the truth can resemble the daunting task of locating a needle in a haystack. Moreover, it is important to acknowledge that our cognitive processes are not always the most dependable guides; they frequently deviate due to cognitive biases, which can result in suboptimal decision-making. Research indicates that managers exhibit biased decision-making more than 50% of the time, which is indeed concerning. Such biases can lead to detrimental outcomes for organizations, including the perpetuation of unfair practices and hindrances to innovation and creativity. However, there is hope. By fostering critical thinking skills, individual can equip their team to challenge assumptions and transcend their inherent biases. This chapter serves as a comprehensive resource for identifying the prevalent biases your team may encounter, elucidating the significance of critical thinking, and exploring effective methods to integrate it into an educational framework.

Critical thinking is contingent upon person's recognition of personal biases. Given the multitude of biases that exist, it is essential to make informed selections. Identify specific biases and seek opportunities within specific plans, group discussions, work assignments, and various interactions amongst people to address and discuss these biases. There are recommendations followed to outline methods to integrate the evaluate of biases into our regular practice, drawing on examples on series of events, Global Changer. If anyone find themselves pondering, "Which biases should they focus on knowing?", this is a decision that only they can make. Consider the most prevalent biases or base their choices on those they have observed in their surroundings.

4.2. Power Behind Critical Thinking Skills

Critical thinking abilities rank among the most sought-after competencies in the job market, with projections from the World Economic Forum indicating that they will be the most desired skill by 2025. However, there is a concerning decline in critical thinking skills globally, particularly among the younger workforce, including Generation Z and millennials. In the current landscape, fostering critical thinking is increasingly vital. The abundance of information readily accessible can lead individuals to quickly search for answers and accept the first result without scrutiny. This overwhelming array of information can foster cognitive biases, undermining our connection to objective facts. Cognitive biases pose significant risks. Organizations that do not prioritize critical thinking are more susceptible to accepting misinformation and making detrimental assumptions influenced by these biases. To remain adaptable in an ever-changing environment, businesses must cultivate a culture of proactive thinkers who can critically assess information and formulate well-informed, balanced conclusions grounded in facts rather than unfounded assumptions. The initial step toward this goal is to enhance awareness. By learning to identify the pitfalls of cognitive biases, individuals can reduce the likelihood of succumbing to them.

Critical Thinking is essential for the integration of thoughts and ideas. It encompasses the incorporation of subjectivity into the cognitive process, facilitating reasoned judgments and leading to well-considered decisions. This concept was examined in the preceding issue. A crucial element of Critical Thinking is the recognition of one's biases and the ability to transcend these biases when making decisions, although this is often more challenging in practice than it is in theory.

4.3. What Are Heuristics?

You may be familiar with the concept of cognitive biases; however, have you encountered the term heuristics? The word heuristics is derived from the Greek term meaning 'to discover' and was introduced in 1974 by researchers Amos Tversky and Daniel Kahneman. Heuristics serve as an adaptive strategy employed by our brains to manage the vast amounts of information encountered daily. These mental shortcuts are based on the knowledge and experiences accumulated by our minds, enabling us to make quick decisions while alleviating cognitive strain. Consequently, our brains efficiently allocate mental resources to other areas that may require greater focus and energy. While heuristics significantly aid our cognitive processes, they can also render us vulnerable to cognitive biases—systematic errors that may result in inaccurate judgments or decisions influenced by non-factual information.

All biases that significantly affect Critical Thinking are categorized as Cognitive Biases. Cognitive bias refers to the tendency to excessively depend on personal beliefs and opinions, which influences one's cognitive processes and reasoning, often leading to flawed judgments and decisions. Numerous biases are classified as cognitive biases, each stemming from distinct origins or reasons. However, they all share a common outcome: they obscure the clarity of thought.

Here, we will examine three prevalent biases that notably impact our thinking:

- **Self-serving Bias**

- **Confirmation Bias**

- **Group Bias**

This section aims to elucidate these biases and their consequences.

Self-Serving Bias This bias involves attributing success or positive outcomes to one's abilities and skills, while negative outcomes are blamed on external factors such as luck. It stems from a deep-seated belief that luck is essential and plays a crucial role in determining results. The negative perception of luck can significantly hinder the effort we invest in tasks. We often hold the belief that, regardless of our actions, luck ultimately dictates the outcome. Overcoming this bias cannot be achieved through a single action or practice. It requires ongoing awareness and accurate assessments. After completing a task, it is beneficial to analyse the results and identify the underlying causes of the outcomes. Conducting such root-cause analyses for both positive and negative results can help establish a connection between our reasoning and the outcomes. It is vital to recognize and confront our flawed reasoning and its effects during this analysis. With consistent learning over time, our belief in luck's influence on results will diminish. A related bias involves an individual's excessive confidence in their abilities.

Confirmation Bias Confirmatory bias refers to the tendency of individuals to filter information, accepting only that which supports their pre-existing beliefs. This phenomenon often occurs unconsciously, as individuals form opinions at the earliest opportunity and subsequently focus solely on evidence that aligns with those opinions, disregarding contradictory information. People are more inclined to listen to those who share their views while ignoring dissenting voices. To mitigate this bias, individuals should actively seek out evidence that challenges their beliefs. Although this may prove difficult initially, consistent practice can enhance this critical skill.

Group Bias Commonly referred to as herd mentality, group bias manifests when individuals are swayed by the majority opinion within their social circles. This form of peer influence significantly impacts decision-making, as social dynamics play a crucial role in shaping choices. For instance, career decisions are frequently influenced by peers, with common stereotypes including professions such as lawyer, engineer, or doctor. Individuals may not consider whether these careers align with their personal interests or passions. A related concept is model bias, where individuals are influenced by their role models or idols. This influence can extend to areas of life where the role model may not be particularly known. For example, if Sachin Tendulkar, a beloved cricketer, expresses a preference for a specific colour / chocolate, one might feel compelled to adopt a liking for that colour/chocolate as well. To counteract this bias, it is essential to return to fundamental questions: What are our true objectives, and what context are we operating within? Are we being unduly influenced by our social group? By objectively evaluating available options and seeking unbiased perspectives, individuals can avoid succumbing to this bias. Like other cognitive biases, overcoming group bias requires conscious effort and practice over time.

4.4. Common Cognitive Biases Types

Let us explore how to identify each type and subsequently examine various strategies for their prevention.

1. **Availability Bias**

Our extensive interactions with the digital realm have rendered us more exposed to information than ever before. A breaking news event or even a trivial rumour can dominate our screens, making us vulnerable to the availability bias.

The availability bias refers to the cognitive shortcut our minds employ when making decisions based on the information that is most readily accessible. This may include a notable or recent event, a significant personal experience, or data influenced by external sources such as media outlets or news reports.

Consider the myriad ways in which you acquire information daily. From televisions and newspapers to smartphones, social media, radio, neighbours, and social circles—the options are virtually limitless.

The impact of the availability bias is exacerbated by our constant connectivity to devices. Two decades ago, our information sources were likely limited to a daily newspaper and the evening news broadcast. Today, however, we are more interconnected than ever. The time spent on screens leads to increased exposure to information, thereby amplifying its potential influence on our perceptions. However, what if the information we encounter on these platforms is itself biased or, even worse, entirely false? As previously noted, new information can be disseminated widely, regardless of its accuracy. Furthermore, when our confirmation bias aligns with this information, we risk accepting potentially harmful or incorrect narratives. The term "fake news" saw a staggering 365% increase in usage between 2016 and 2017, and research indicates that 42.8% of individuals acknowledge sharing misleading news stories.

2. **Media bias**

Contemporary news narratives tend to prioritize those stories that feature the most striking and emotionally charged headlines, often sensationalizing content to enhance its emotional impact. Media bias is defined as the inclination exhibited by journalists and news producers in their reporting and coverage of events.

Our news outlets/channels frequently emphasize negative or sensational stories, leading the public to perceive this as a faithful representation of reality, when in fact, it merely offers a limited perspective.

The consequences of selective reporting can be significant. A study has demonstrated that the public tends to overestimate their risk of certain cancers that receive more media attention, while underestimating those that are less frequently reported. This misperception can adversely affect individual behavior and health management practices.

3. **The Framing Effect**

Framing refers to the manner in which the presentation of choices in various contexts, situations, and terminologies influences our understanding of the information provided.

This phenomenon is pervasive and subtly influences our views of others, occasionally leading to detrimental judgments or stereotypes.

Such bias can be observed in media portrayals of specific groups, the connections they draw, or the terminology employed. For instance, young people are frequently characterized with descriptors like entitled, lazy, and irresponsible, which contributes to a negative societal perception of the younger generation.

4. **AI Bias**

As our dependence on artificial intelligence continues to grow, it raises concerns about the potential for bias within these digital assistants. Contrary to the common perception of AI as neutral, it can inadvertently exacerbate existing biases.

This phenomenon occurs because programs like ChatGPT rely on data and information provided by humans. If the data input contains biases, the AI perpetuates these biases by consistently reproducing the flawed information, thereby influencing our perceptions and contributing to the dissemination of inaccuracies.

Recent studies, including one conducted by the University of East Anglia, have indicated that ChatGPT exhibits a political bias, showing a preference for left-leaning ideologies.

Understanding the various types of biases is crucial, as it allows us to recognize those that render us especially susceptible to errors. Once these biases are identified, actively working to address them over time can enhance our decision-making abilities and reduce the impact of these biases on our choices. Seeking guidance from mentors to pinpoint these biases, along with utilizing mind-mapping to document our thought processes, are effective practices that provide valuable insights and illustrate our progress in a constructive manner.

4.5. Grow Critical Thinking Skills

Upon recognizing our vulnerability to cognitive biases, it may feel as though we are traversing a precarious path, striving to maintain equilibrium in our objective assessments while resisting the pull of our habitual subjective reasoning. The process of forming our own opinions can often resemble swimming against a strong current, with torrents of information attempting to divert us in various directions. Nevertheless, there exists a significant empowerment in reclaiming authority over our judgments and reestablishing the art of independent thought. The essence of this endeavour lies in the practice of critical thinking. As we cultivate our critical thinking abilities, we diminish the influence of unconscious biases on our judgments and viewpoints. Any scientist is well-acquainted with the concept of critical appraisal — a systematic approach to analysing and evaluating conclusions to ascertain the validity and reliability of findings. If we could metaphorically apply a magnifying glass to our cognitive processes and meticulously examine our own judgments, we might succeed in mitigating the impact of our biases.

Steps to Enhance Your Critical Thinking Abilities

1. **Inquire/Question**

Inquiring is fundamental to the process of critical thinking. Albert Einstein once remarked, "The important thing is to not stop questioning. Curiosity has its own reason for existing." Take a moment to reflect on your beliefs and evaluations. Where do they originate? Is there substantial evidence supporting them? What influences might be at play? Distinguish between assumptions and facts. Allocate time to determine which evaluations may require reconsideration.

2. **Assess and Scrutinize** incoming information thoroughly, keeping essential questions in mind. Is the source credible? Are there any perspectives that are absent? What alternative interpretations exist for this information? Similar to cautiously testing the stability of ice before committing your full weight, critically evaluate the information before forming any conclusions or opinions.

3. **Stay Open-Minded** This entails considering information from various perspectives, sources, and viewpoints. A diverse array of information is crucial for developing a well-rounded judgment.

4. **Engage in Active Listening** Hone your active listening abilities. Approach conversations with an open mind, setting aside preconceived judgments and assumptions. This practice will enable you to incorporate a wide range of opinions and diverse perspectives.

5. **Cultivate Awareness** Begin to attune yourself to the workings of your mind. Cognitive biases can create a background noise that we often overlook. By recognizing what your biases are, you can begin to address them. The positive aspect is that you have already initiated this important first step!

Four Effective Exercises to Enhance Team's Critical Thinking Abilities

The following are four effective exercises that can be implemented:

1. **Team Collaboration** Facilitate weekly collaboration sessions within the team. Establish a psychologically safe atmosphere that encourages open discussions and the sharing of ideas, which will lead to a rich exchange of diverse perspectives and insights.

2. **Argument Mapping** Identify the primary assumption or argument being presented. For instance, consider a straightforward assertion such as "our target audience primarily consists of 30-year-old females." Create a visual representation of the assumptions, sources, and supporting rationale for this argument. Assess its robustness and validity, and make necessary adjustments to your assumption based on this assessment.

3. **Socratic Questioning** This technique, developed by the ancient Greek philosopher Socrates, emphasizes that genuine wisdom arises from acknowledging the limits of our knowledge and actively seeking diverse viewpoints. The method employs open-ended questions to scrutinize assumptions.

Examples of such questions include:

What leads me to hold this belief?

What evidence substantiates my viewpoint?

What alternative perspectives exist?

What assumptions have I made?

What consequences arise from my judgment?

4.**Escape Echo Chambers**

Broaden the news and social media consumption to encompass a variety of informational sources. Consider starting with: The Happy Newspaper: This digital platform is dedicated to delivering uplifting news stories that highlight positive occurrences around the globe. Humans of New York: This website shares the narratives of numerous individuals in New York City, emphasizing the significance of recognizing that everyone has a unique story and the necessity of challenging preconceived notions. Reuters: An impartial news outlet that prioritizes fact-based reporting from a diverse array of journalists worldwide, advocating for the importance of an informed public.

4.6. Key Takeaways

In today's highly digitalized environment, the vast amount of information available to us increases our vulnerability to cognitive biases, especially availability bias. The digital platforms we utilize for information can also be biased or misleading. Common examples of cognitive biases include the framing effect, confirmation bias, and availability bias. One effective method to identify and mitigate cognitive biases is through the practice of critical thinking. Fostering critical thinking skills among team members can lead to improved business results, including enhanced decision-making, greater creativity and innovation, and the creation of a psychologically safe workplace.

Part 5: Framework And Models

5.1. What to Learn?

In this chapter, we present a straightforward framework designed to assist individuals in navigating the critical thinking process. This framework, which offers various tools and techniques, is comprised of three essential components: clarity, conclusions, and decisions.

The realm of creativity, critical thinking serves as a formidable instrument that can unveil new opportunities and improve your problem-solving skills. By comprehending and utilizing the essence of critical thinking, anyone can tackle challenges with a lucid and analytical perspective.

5.2. Critical Thinking Essential for Creativity

Critical thinking is essential for nurturing creativity. It enables individuals to tackle problems and challenges from various perspectives, prompting them to look beyond superficial solutions and explore alternative approaches. By questioning established beliefs and scrutinizing current ideas, critical thinking paves the way for new opportunities and fosters innovation.

Engaging in critical thinking enhances one's ability to identify connections among seemingly disparate concepts and encourages unconventional thinking. This cognitive adaptability allows for the generation of novel ideas, the exploration of diverse viewpoints, and the creative resolution of issues.

Furthermore, critical thinking equips individuals to assess the practicality and efficacy of their ideas. By rigorously evaluating their own thoughts and acknowledging potential limitations or challenges, individuals can refine and enhance their creative solutions. This iterative process of assessment and improvement is vital for converting innovative concepts into actionable and successful results.

By developing critical thinking abilities, one can improve their mental frameworks and cognitive structures, facilitating a more organized and analytical approach to creative projects. Critical thinking empowers individuals to question assumptions, consider various viewpoints, and make informed decisions to realize their creative aspirations. As we further explore critical thinking frameworks and their relevance to creativity, you will uncover how these frameworks can assist in problem-solving, idea generation, and the enhancement of analytical capabilities. Let us proceed in our exploration of unlocking your cognitive potential by examining various critical thinking models.

5.3. Critical Thinking Models

These models offer frameworks and strategies that enable people to tackle challenges from multiple perspectives. In this section, we will explore the RED Model of critical thinking, which comprises three essential elements: Recognize Assumptions, Evaluate Arguments, and Draw Conclusions.

The RED Model

Recognize Assumptions

The recognition of assumptions is a fundamental aspect of critical thinking. Assumptions represent the unspoken beliefs and ideas that shape our thoughts and behaviours. By making these assumptions explicit, one can evaluate their validity and relevance to the current context.

To identify assumptions, it is necessary to scrutinize the information presented and uncover any implicit biases or preconceived ideas that may affect your reasoning. By questioning these assumptions, you can explore new avenues and expand your viewpoint, facilitating more innovative and creative problem-solving.

Evaluate Arguments

Evaluating arguments entails a thorough assessment of the reasoning and evidence that support a specific claim or perspective. It is crucial to analyse the logical framework of an argument and the reliability of the evidence provided. This process enables you to discern the strengths and weaknesses of the argument, leading to informed conclusions.

To effectively evaluate arguments, one should examine the credibility of the sources, the pertinence of the evidence, and the logical consistency of the reasoning. By critically assessing arguments, you can uncover flaws, identify gaps in reasoning, and recognize potential biases, thereby enhancing your decision-making and the development of well-founded ideas.

Draw Conclusions

The final step in the RED Model is drawing conclusions. This process involves synthesizing information, assessing the evidence, and arriving at a reasoned judgment or decision. By concluding, you reinforce your understanding of the situation and establish a clear stance or course of action.

In drawing conclusions, it is essential to weigh the strengths and weaknesses of the arguments, evaluate the quality of the evidence, and consider the implications of any assumptions. This approach allows you to reach well-supported conclusions grounded in critical analysis and thoughtful consideration.

By utilizing the RED Model of critical thinking, you can improve your capacity to recognize assumptions, evaluate arguments, and draw informed conclusions.

The SCAMPER Framework

The SCAMPER framework serves as an effective tool for fostering creative thinking, capable of igniting innovative ideas and solutions. Each letter in the acronym signifies a distinct method for generating new opportunities. Below, we will examine each component of the SCAMPER framework:

Substitute

This phase involves contemplating the substitution of one aspect of a problem or concept with an alternative. Pose the question, "What can I replace or substitute to gain a new perspective?" By implementing substitutions, you may reveal novel insights and potential enhancements.

Combine

The letter "C" in SCAMPER denotes combine. This phase prompts you to explore how various elements or ideas can be integrated or fused to create something original. Consider how you might amalgamate concepts or features to develop unique solutions or methodologies.

Adapt

Adaptation focuses on modifying existing ideas, processes, or products to align with a different context or objective. Reflect on the question, "How can I alter or adjust this to suit another situation?" Through adaptation, you can discover innovative methods to repurpose current resources or concepts.

Modify

The letter "M" in SCAMPER signifies modify, which entails making alterations or adjustments to an existing idea or product. Contemplate how you can refine or enhance specific aspects to boost performance or functionality. This phase encourages critical thinking regarding the details and the refinement of your ideas.

Put to Another Use

In this phase, you investigate how an idea or product can be utilized in a different manner. Consider alternative applications or scenarios where a particular concept or item may hold value. By exploring various uses, you can unveil hidden potential and inventive solutions.

Eliminate

To cultivate new ideas, it is essential to contemplate what can be eliminated. Ask yourself, "What can I remove or reduce to simplify the concept or issue?" By discarding unnecessary elements or steps, you can streamline processes and discover more efficient solutions.

Rearrange

The concluding phase of the SCAMPER framework involves rearranging elements or components.

The Six Thinking Hats Framework

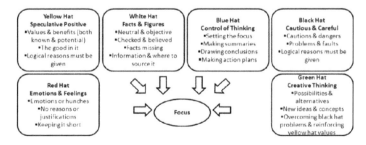

The Six Thinking Hats Framework serves as an effective instrument for enhancing critical thinking and facilitating decision-making processes. Created by Edward de Bono, this framework prompts individuals to adopt various perspectives or "hats" when addressing a problem or situation. Each hat symbolizes a distinct mode of thought, aiding in the examination of different facets of the issue at hand. Below is a detailed examination of each hat:

White Hat Thinking

Adopting the White Hat entails concentrating on the collection and analysis of information. This approach involves scrutinizing the facts, data, and objective elements pertinent to the problem or situation. White Hat thinking prioritizes objectivity and rationality by assessing what is known and identifying the information necessary for making well-informed decisions.

Red Hat Thinking

The Red Hat embodies emotions and intuition. When donning this hat, individuals are encouraged to articulate their feelings and instinctive reactions without the necessity for logical justification. Red Hat thinking facilitates the exploration of personal emotions, viewpoints, and intuitions, which may yield valuable insights that extend beyond mere logical analysis.

Black Hat Thinking

The Black Hat denotes critical evaluation and caution. This mode of thought involves assessing potential risks, vulnerabilities, and disadvantages associated with various ideas or solutions. Black Hat thinking is instrumental in pinpointing possible challenges and obstacles, allowing for a thorough evaluation of the viability and effectiveness of different alternatives.

Yellow Hat Thinking

Yellow Hat thinking emphasizes optimism, positivity, and potential benefits. When utilizing the Yellow Hat, individuals investigate the possible advantages, benefits, and opportunities that ideas or solutions may offer. This mode of thought encourages consideration of the value and favourable outcomes that can emerge from diverse perspectives.

Green Hat Thinking

The Green Hat symbolizes creativity and innovation. This mode of thinking inspires individuals to explore novel ideas, generate alternatives, and engage in unconventional thinking. Green Hat thinking encompasses brainstorming, lateral thinking, and the acceptance of unique approaches to problem-solving.

The context of nurturing creativity, the utilization of critical thinking models proves to be exceptionally advantageous. These frameworks offer systematic methods for addressing problems, solving decisions, and generating ideas, as to improving analytical capabilities and broadening creative possibilities. Experts keeps on continiously examine the application of critical thinking models across various facets of the creative process.

5.4. Key Takeaways

To enhance our critical thinking abilities and unlock our creative potential, it's important to cultivate certain skills and habits. By practicing reflection and self-analysis, seeking diverse perspectives, and challenging assumptions and biases, individual can develop a strong foundation for effective critical thinking. To expand cognitive horizons and foster creativity, it is essential to actively pursue a variety of observations. Engage in discussions with individuals from diverse backgrounds, cultures, and fields of expertise. Pay close attention to their insights and reflect on their reasoning. By immersing self in a range of viewpoints, can confront our own assumptions and biases, ultimately resulting in more comprehensive and innovative thought processes. It is important to enter these dialogues with an open mind and a genuine eagerness to learn.

Glossary of Key Terms in Critical Thinking

I. Critical Thinking: The process of analyzing, evaluating, and synthesizing information to make reasoned judgments and decisions, often involving questioning assumptions and considering alternative perspectives.

II. Analysis: The process of breaking down complex information or issues into smaller, manageable parts to understand their structure and relationships.

III. Evaluation: The act of assessing evidence and arguments' credibility, relevance, and strength to form a reasoned judgment or conclusion.

IV. Inference: The logical process of drawing conclusions based on evidence and reasoning, moving from premises to a reasoned judgment.

V. Reasoning: The cognitive process of thinking logically and systematically to form judgments, make decisions, or solve problems.

VI. Bias: A predisposition or prejudice that affects objective analysis and can lead to skewed or unfair judgments, impacting reasoning accuracy.

VII. Assumption: An underlying belief or premise that is taken for granted without proof, which can affect the validity of arguments and conclusions.

VIII. Argument: A set of statements or reasons put forward to support a conclusion or viewpoint, often consisting of premises and a conclusion.

IX. Premise: A statement or proposition that provides the foundation for an argument, from which a conclusion is drawn.

X. Critical Reflection: The process of carefully and systematically considering one's own beliefs, values, and reasoning processes to enhance understanding and decision-making.

Milton Keynes UK
Ingram Content Group UK Ltd.
UKHW050442201124
451264UK00014B/225